Malibu Diary

Environmental Arts and Humanities Series

Malibu Diary

Notes from an Urban Refugee

. . . .

PENELOPE GRENOBLE O'MALLEY

UNIVERSITY OF NEVADA PRESS
Reno & Las Vegas

Environmental Arts and Humanities Series
Series Editors: Scott Slovic and Michael P. Cohen

University of Nevada Press, Reno, Nevada 89557 USA
Copyright ©2004 by University of Nevada Press
All rights reserved
Manufactured in the United States of America
Design by Barbara Jellow
Library of Congress Cataloging-in-Publication Data
O'Malley, Penelope Grenoble.
Malibu diary : notes from an urban refugee / Penelope Grenoble
O'Malley.
p. cm. — (Environmental arts and humanities series)
Includes bibliographical references (p.   ).
ISBN 0-87417-566-6 (alk. paper)
1. O'Malley, Penelope Grenoble. 2. Malibu Region (Calif.)—Biography.
3. Malibu Region (Calif.)—Environmental conditions. 4. Malibu Region
(Calif.)—Description and travel. 5. Wilderness
areas—California—Malibu Region. 6. Natural
history—California—Malibu Region. 7. Environmental
protection—California—Malibu Region. 8. Cities and
towns—California—Growth—Case studies. I. Title. II. Series.
F869.M27043 2004
917.94'94—dc22   2003017450
The paper used in this book meets the requirements of American National Standard for
Information Sciences—Permanence of Paper for Printed Library Materials, ANSI z.48-1984.
Binding materials were selected for strength and durability.
First Printing
13 12 11 10 09 08 07 06 05 04
5 4 3 2 1

For Margaret

. . . . .

· · · · ·

When we start deceiving ourselves into thinking not
that we want something or need something ... but
that it is a moral imperative that we have it, then is
when we join the fashionable madmen.

JOAN DIDION, *On Morality*

CONTENTS

· · · · · · · · · ·

ex urbanis   1

The Journey Out   13

Blowin' Smoke   32

Cowboys and Indians:
   A Drama in Three Acts   51

Wasting Time   71

Wisdom in Solstice Canyon   92

On the Fence   109

The Days the Rains Came   133

Long Way Home   156

More News from the Front   173

DATA   183

SOURCES AND ACKNOWLEDGMENTS   185

Malibu Diary

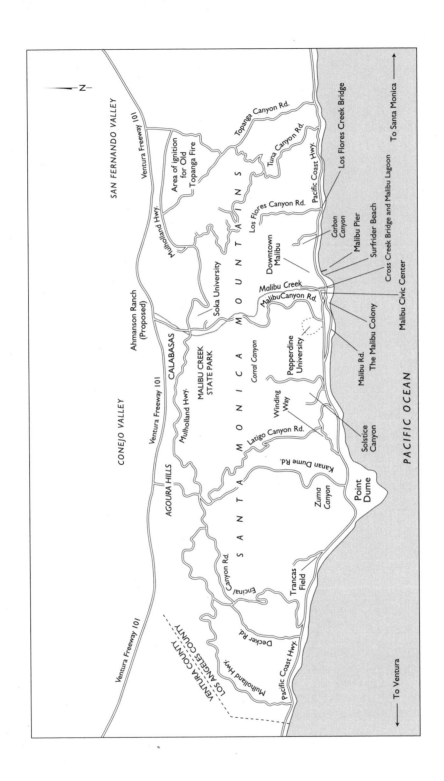

ex urbanis

. . . .

I walked up the gravel path not because I wanted to but because it looked like the fastest way to get away from the houses and onto open land. Nothing smells here, which surprises me. In the cold predawn air, the November wind burns harsh against my skin—a relief, actually, after the buttoned-up heat of the hotel room these past four days.

At the end of the path a huge steel-beam cross looks across the bowl of the town to the desert beyond. I stop to watch the rising sun cast its pink glow across the top of the mountains; no smells yet, though, and only a vague hope looms across a dirt trail that wanders up the hill past the menacing cross. Anything to escape.

I follow the switchbacks to where the trail dead-ends in a paved cul-de-sac, stop to watch three jackrabbits forage in a patch of sparse brush, and allow my eye to be drawn to a heavy bronze plaque bolted on a granite boulder. The rabbits scatter, a youngster first, then an adolescent, its tail barely white, then a creaky grandparent that arches stiffly away from me. I turn from the boulder without reading the plaque and follow the rabbits down an arroyo that cuts through a small mesa off to my right and the promise of more open land. I walk north, stop when I hear highway noise, then turn east until finally there are no houses and no cars. The edge of the path is littered with beer bottles, an empty

Marlboro pack, a fragment of jockey shorts—obviously I am not the first one here. I follow the path to where it stops at the edge of the mesa and look out across the canyon where I see a row of new houses winding along a ribbon of fresh asphalt, some just finished and covered with a coat of stucco tinted to look like adobe, some framed in raw wood, which I know is not the way you build an adobe house.

I turn around and head back the way I came, cross yet another path and follow it down another arroyo and up the other side. On top again, I stop to check the sun, but my gaze is jarred by movement in my peripheral vision. Two dogs, a hound and a German shepherd, wander down a paved driveway from a large house, mansion-size compared to the houses I saw below. This mansion is constructed in the same faux adobe as the houses in the subdivision but with decks and picture windows, Anglo twists meant to appeal to the urban refugees who are edging out the Hispano majority in this place. I look down, and directly in front of me I see a piece of raw wood cut to a point at the top: a surveyor's stake. I am standing on a building pad one arroyo away from the mansion with the driveway and the dogs. I suspect the open ground I have been walking and perhaps even the park with its overbearing cross are concessions of open space extracted from a developer in exchange for these mesa lots.

This is Santa Fe, New Mexico, not southern California where I live—but it happens whenever enough people decide to make a run for it.

The it I am speaking about—the dynamic that concerns me—occurs when enough of us get tired of living in cities and decamp to a small town or resort community or some "out-of-the-way place" that has managed to maintain what is attractive about its setting and character. We say we're drawn to such places by the atmosphere of small-town living we find absent in cities, that we want to live where people know each other, and day-to-day life is more manageable. We say we want to live where people care about each other. In places like Santa Fe we usually mention the scenery and how we enjoy living close to nature. We say we're motivated to keep our scale of living small and inclined to protect the natural landscape, holy ground now that it is so close at hand. Except that it is often the land that suffers, parceled out for subdivisions and shopping centers, for schools and office buildings, the whole range of civic improvements we can't seem to bring ourselves to leave behind.

I have lived in Los Angeles almost as long as I have been an adult. I have friends here. I have finally determined what to wear in winter and during February's false spring. I have learned that when the leaves on the sycamore trees in Beverly Hills begin to crinkle, it's time to start thinking about Thanksgiving and the encroaching winter dark. I have discovered the best way to get around the city and the most expedient means by which I might leave L.A. behind, although always temporarily, and always with the thought that someday my escape would be permanent. During all my years in Los Angeles, probably not one twelve-month flip of the calendar has been accomplished without my thinking I would leave. Convinced my city sojourn was temporary, I made excuses—my husband's job, my job, obligations. I told myself I was in transition and that I would get on with the real business of my life once I had established myself in the right place for good. But even with the husband gone and many of the obligations satisfied, I still hadn't managed enough momentum to leave. "I've tried to think of some place to go," I told friends who nodded in agreement. "But I can't think of anywhere better than here."

What was this sense, then, that it was just a matter of time before I was gone for good? And gone from what? This was also vague. Gone, I thought, from what I don't like about cities, which is that they are large, with too many people and too little sunlight, too few trees. The fact that Los Angeles is constantly changing, which makes it difficult to feel that once settled, you are home. But where would I go if I decided to leave? This was also confusing. A place, I thought, where I could see mountains and sea and sky, where I could be *away*. Again the question: away from what? Back then the demons were more easily identified: too much noise and congestion, too much concrete.

I wish I could say that I woke up one morning and realized that if I didn't do something soon, I was stuck in L.A. jeopardizing whatever opportunities still awaited me, but things never happen to me that way, the sudden "aha" followed by a moment of insight. I have to work at it. Which means the realization that I had spent over two decades in Los Angeles and still wasn't comfortable didn't come so much as a surprise as a disappointment. During the years I attempted to make L.A. home, I lived in eight different neighborhoods, from the townhouse my husband and I rented in Culver City to a house of my own near Beverly Hills. With each move I was certain the dream had finally been caged, nailed down—until recently, when I had to admit time was running out. Unless I found a place where I could be comfortable soon, all I would have to fall back on after twenty years in southern California was a ragged series of stops and starts.

There was also the question of what I had sought when I left the East Coast for the West. What had I gained or lost moving across the country? California had meant to me what it has meant to millions who arrived before me and others who still come, the Forty-Niners looking to get rich quick, land-poor immigrants from the Midwest hoping for jobs, a continuing stream of sick and disabled searching for relief in the climate. The Filipinos and Persians, Koreans, and Vietnamese who still come, each with a different vision for their new home.

As a child I dreamed of being a cowgirl, no, a park ranger, sun-baked and healthy. In California I thought I would write: a novel, no, poetry. No, a book about cougars. So it was that when I finally decided to pull up stakes and leave L.A. for good, I wasn't sure what I wanted to do once I got where I was going. I was forever looking north across the city to the green reef of the Santa Monica Mountains, forever wishing on snow-capped Mt. Baldy or the long offshore curve of Catalina, sparkling on a clear January morning. I had no idea the restlessness I felt couldn't be satisfied in a single bound or that at bottom it was the need to be one with a place in ways I hadn't yet the insight to imagine.

When I finally decided to pack my bags and leave for good, my escape was only forty minutes up the southern California coast to Malibu, close enough to the city that I could sneak back when the spirit moved me but far enough away to feel I had, in fact, escaped. My plan was to isolate myself, and given that the ten thousand or so people who lived in

Malibu back then were spread out along twenty-seven miles of coast, it appeared this wouldn't be difficult. A stone's throw from the long roll of the Pacific Ocean, backdropped by a range of rugged mountains, I would break free of my frustrations. Inspired by Malibu's dramatic natural setting, I would move on with my life.

The geography that makes Malibu scenic is a product of the gradual westward swing of the Santa Monica Mountains away from the Los Angeles basin toward the sea. One enters this hallowed ground along narrow, heaving Pacific Coast Highway, which hugs the ocean so tightly here there's barely enough room for four lanes of traffic. Like other communities that have established themselves in isolated settings, Malibu (*The* Malibu as real estate broker Louis Busch described it back in the 1940s) lacks a mass transportation link with the outside world. There's no ferry to Santa Monica thirteen highway miles to the east, no public transport of any sort unless you count the MTA buses that deliver our nannies and housekeepers in the morning. Back in those more idealistic forties, a forward-thinking booster went out on a limb to establish a private bus line to connect Malibu with the rest of southern California. But even with eighteen trips a day back and forth to Santa Monica, Shoreline Transit fizzled, a victim of the community's impulse for isolation.

The exile I imagined for myself was centered on the house I rented at the far western edge of Malibu on Point Dume, a peninsula of bluff-top land that was once planned for a polo field and a handful of equestrian estates but instead materialized into a neighborhood of aspiring middle-class families. This high south-facing v forms the far western curve of Santa Monica Bay, where it sweeps north from Long Beach past Santa Monica and juts far enough out to sea that the Chumash used the Point to navigate and the federal government once planned a lighthouse to safeguard coastal shipping. Smugglers have landed everything from illegal Chinese laborers to Prohibition booze along the isolated beaches in Point Dume's lee. As late as 1966, *The Malibu Times* was reporting a bust of $500,000 worth of marijuana dumped overboard in seabags, enough of the illegal weed to fill the sheriff's office in the old courthouse clear to the ceiling.

When I left Los Angeles for Malibu after almost ten years of shilly-shallying around, I was at a juncture in my life that appeared to offer promise as long as I didn't mind an occasional wild turn around a blind corner. I was divorced and between jobs, which seemed to make it as good a time as any to test the supposition that I would be better off living on my own away from the city. (I was wrong in one respect—in Malibu I met a man equally inclined toward isolation and we married.) I took as models for my exile Georgia O'Keeffe and California writer-naturalist Mary Austin, two women who seemed at home in hostile landscapes. I had read *Desert Solitaire*, Edward Abbey's ode to self-imposed exile, and I was familiar with the long tradition of writers and artists who sought their muses along Malibu's coast.

When I moved to Malibu in 1986, I knew little of the landscape I hoped would inspire me—who owned it or what manner of flora and fauna it might support—and truth be known I wasn't much interested. Nor did I give much thought to the other people who had settled here or why we had all ended up in the same place. I took for granted the mountains that protect Malibu from development should stay the way they are, and I agreed with the attitude I heard around town, and at my new friend Hana's dining room table, that there was no reason to give in to this kind of pressure. I knew nothing of these mountains that cut Malibu off from the subdivisions edging out of the San Fernando Valley—how high they are (three thousand feet) or that I could spend the better part of a day crossing them on foot. I could not have told you that most of the land in Malibu slopes so steeply toward the ocean that if it snowed, we could ski. Likewise, I was unaware that I had taken up residence among the rarest of the earth's vegetation, Mediterranean broadleaf evergreen forest, and that the hillsides I saw from my kitchen window were home to some five hundred species of wildlife and over half that number of birds. I was unaware my new home was situated amid an intricate web of forty watersheds and that if I took the time to explore, I would discover valuable specimens of fast-disappearing California oak woodland and sycamore savannah. I knew nothing of the seventy civic agencies that protected all this or that the Santa Monica Mountains anchor what the National Park Service likes to call this country's largest "urban park."

Such lapses aside, when I moved to Malibu, I considered myself an environmentalist. Which meant that I decried the conscription of what remained of southern California's landscape for shopping malls and subdivisions, that I objected to dumping sewage or any other human-generated debris into streams, lakes, or the ocean, and was against the clearing of Brazil's rainforests, the Japanese slaughter of whales, and the Western world's dependence on fossil fuels. I recycled what I could, used sponges instead of paper towels, and washed my clothes with phosphate-free detergent. But mine was environmentalism in absentia. I had never been called upon to demonstrate my idealism in any way that seriously inconvenienced me or to defend my views with anyone other than people I knew were predisposed to agree with me. I had behind me three years editing the *Los Angeles Free Press,* which once dominated what was called underground journalism on the West Coast, and a stint at *Westways,* the Southern California Automobile Club's culture and lifestyle magazine, where the editorial policy was as nonconfrontationally benign as the *Freep's* was in-your-face. Sorting through underreported stories in southern California at *Westways,* I discovered the Santa Catalina Island Conservancy, a private nonprofit foundation established to protect the island from development. Soon enough I had abandoned my desk in downtown Los Angeles for Catalina's remote interior.

During my first years in Malibu, I commuted. My job was in the city, most of my friends still lived in Los Angeles, and L.A. was the place to shop, see a film, and get something good to eat. Five years into this arrangement, things changed. Convinced we were under siege from development, terrified our way of life was in danger, we residents of Malibu declared our independence from Los Angeles County, which had provided what government we'd had for the past sixty years. Although it was obvious the community was being threatened by an expansion-minded board of supervisors and their friends among developers who saw potential in our mountains and foothills (and cared little whether their version of growth was what we imagined), like most of those who voted for incorporation, I hadn't given much thought to what it would mean to be independent of county managers, only that the 120,000 new residents the expansionist-minded supervisors had in mind for Malibu was outrageous and couldn't be sustained. I had no idea where the money to run a local government would come from or how such a government would provide essential services. But even as I began to understand the scope of what we had undertaken, I thought that left to our own devices and in close contact with one another, we would succeed, that we might even become a "lighthouse" for communities elsewhere facing similar challenges, as city council candidate Mary Kay Kamath had once put it.

The fact is that when I left Los Angeles for Malibu, I still carried with me some pretty shaky notions about the communal good feeling I expected to discover unfolding full flower in a small town. I anticipated that since there were so few of us living here and we had chosen this place for similar reasons, we would work together to achieve our vision for the community. I imagined we might weave ourselves together into a whole cloth, pull the stitches tight, and so repel anyone who attempted entry at some point of self-interest. I assumed that because the town was small and our government was now in our midst, our leaders would be subject to swift and immediate accountability. And since so many of us were newcomers and starting fresh, we would be relieved of tearing down what was old and outdated before we could begin anew. We had dislodged the slovenly boarder who cooked cabbage in his room; now we would clean and paint, then sit on the porch rocking for a while in the evening breeze.

Likewise, I had no idea I was heading toward one of those blind corners when I signed on as a reporter for *The Malibu Times*. I was unaware the paper I had chosen was considered prodevelopment by many people in the community while the town's other weekly was solidly slow growth. I had no idea that by accepting the job as the newspaper's one full-time reporter, I would be scorned as a turncoat by many in town and cheered as a voice of reason by as many others as I watched events unfold firsthand. I listened as Malibu's new city council debated the protection of migrating monarch butterflies until three in the morning while roads slid down canyons and potholes multiplied on Pacific Coast Highway. I drank coffee at homeowners association meetings, trudged flooded streets in hip boots, and followed firefighters into the flames. Individual activists and groups focused on a particular issue were not likely to appreciate the patterns that emerged as Malibu attempted to govern itself, but moving from one hot spot to another, I saw it all. People stopped me in the supermarket and stashed purloined documents in my mailbox, and when they didn't like what I wrote, they told me to my face. Driving up and down PCH, keeping track of the issues that galvanized the community, everywhere the theme repeated itself: development is bad for people, slow growth is good for communities like ours. I was embarrassed when I recognized a similar inflexibility in my own thinking.

Were slow growth and environmental protection allies as I supposed, so that when a community moves to slow growth it automatically protects its natural environment? And does this mean the impulse to protect the earth from the effects of our human consumption goes hand in hand with defending one's home ground against yet another subdivision or chain store? Or is one concept servant to the other, so that environmental protection is but one element in the grander scheme of slow growth? Do people who discover that a hillside of toyon or mountain lilac is important to their quality of life rush to trade in their leaking septic tanks and hook up to a state-of-the-art sewage treatment facility? Or is this connection too vague?

I had no idea I had been seduced by the scenery when I settled in Malibu or how much was going on beneath the surface that offered more solid opportunities for the enlightenment I had in mind. As a journalist I was confined to the facts, but as a citizen of the town I covered, I couldn't help but filter the events I reported through the skin of my own opinions. Many of us in Malibu liked to think of ourselves as the last bastion of resistance, keeping the wolves of development at bay. I suspect there is both hypocrisy and self-deception in this view. Standing on our right to live where we want in the way we please, with the physical limitations of our natural setting guaranteeing our determination—and assuming little responsibility to ameliorate the effects of our having settled here, or the difficulties we've left behind—we suggest that anyone so inclined should have like opportunity. In this sense Malibu may be less a lighthouse than a warning beacon, a community located in a dramatic natural setting close enough to a large city to be attractive, but where buildable land is scarce and the landscape fragile. Because the Santa Monica Mountains squeeze so close to the ocean here, old-timers and newcomers alike have moved farther and farther onto outlying steep hillsides and into canyon-bottom floodplains where they not only put themselves at risk from the natural processes that have shaped this place, but at the same time threaten the well-being of the area's natural inhabitants. Aside from escape, there is no reason for Malibu and communities like it to exist. There's no industry and little commerce, and unlike Santa Barbara farther up the coast, Malibu has always been wary of outsiders and uncomfortable thinking of itself as a vacation community. There is the further consideration that many of us urban expatriates who have settled here are attracted less by the landscape than by the opportunity to flee what we find uncomfortable about city living.

When trauma makes an appearance the normal routine of life is interrupted. There is no doubt the community I encountered on the fringe of L.A.'s sprawl was traumatized, first by the threat of unwise development, then by the choices we made to protect ourselves. Before I moved to Malibu, I never imagined I would sympathize with someone with plans to build a shopping center two blocks from the ocean, or that I would support the interests of a wealthy Anglo over a band of Native Americans. I never thought I would become impatient with take-charge people.

I made several attempts to make sense of what I encountered when I ran away to Malibu, but it was not until I began to link what I covered as a reporter with how I felt about what had happened during the time I spent along this isolated stretch of southern California's coast that I became acquainted with the degree to which my own worldview had been shaken. The perspective I offer will be unfamiliar, especially to those whose idea of Malibu has been primed by the false drama of fires and floods, or nurtured by the same illusions of escape I myself found so attractive. For my own part, I hope never again to burden a place with such shallow expectations.

We begin, then, with the appeal of the landscape, the rugged, chaparral-covered sandstone, the rolling, unbroken expanse of azure sea, and the calm these inspire, a sense of being made one with something beyond oneself in a setting that nurtures solitude. Although I had planned to live apart in Malibu, early in my exile I fell in with a group of regulars who gathered to drink wine at the home of a woman who played the role of the neighborhood matriarch. At Hana's table I found the sense of community I had missed in the city, and I began to think my dream of being one with a place might be accomplished. But what if, as well as being beguiling, this landscape I found so attractive could also betray me? Other circumstances suggested further cause for distress. What if I allowed my virtue, in regard to the natural environment, to be conscripted toward more selfish ends? What if the natural barriers that make it difficult for people to settle in Malibu also cut me off from opportunities to be part of something larger? What if instead of moving purposefully toward a new way of life, I was in fact running away?

We all dream of home, past homes we've lost, future homes that elude us, how we might make whatever place we presently inhabit the most like home. In the developed world we focus our longing on structures, modern versions of Old World mansions, stylized country cottages and lakeside cabins we labor to furnish according to prescribed images. Our goal is to live a lifestyle—as if we can't figure out for ourselves what makes us comfortable. We borrow analogies from nature and call those places to which we escape our "nest" or "roost" or "perch," from which we boldly sally forth to take our place in the world. Home is real: town house, ranch house, tract house, beach cabin. Home is also symbolic, our refuge, retreat, port in a storm. Being at home is our collective longing, a place where we feel we are in our element, at journey's end. When we say home, we also mean security, safety, comfort and warmth. When we think of our relationship with the individual piece of ground we inhabit, we think of how we live on it—our garden, our swimming pool, the children's sandbox and swing set. When these fail to satisfy, we enlarge our horizons and speak of our territory, our place, in the sense that a biologist might refer to a creature's habitat or range. Home is a place where we feel good.

I went to Malibu like many others. Attracted by the climate and lifestyle, I thought I wanted a place where I could live close to nature and away from the city. Without realizing it, I also longed to be part of a community of people with whom I shared common values. I was looking for a place to *be*. I discovered none of this is easy. Not uncovering the self I sought here, nor establishing a life that would be authentic. I came to realize the inner hum I searched for was indeed attached to this environment and the particular fig leaf it wears (*ex urbanis*). I also discovered that lifestyle, no matter how attractively turned out, is a poor substitute for an authentic life well lived, and how much fear of loss can constrict and bind. I learned that my place to be is inside myself, and I a turtle with my house on my back.

The Journey Out

. . . .

Oh . . . to see no envious faces, no saddened eyes; to see or
hear no unkind look or word! To absorb the peace the
hills have, to drink in the charm of the brook, and
to receive the strength of the mountains . . .

Frederick Hastings Rindge, *Happy Days in Southern California*

1979–1986

When you drove out to Malibu in those days, the journey unraveled in
stages. The road gradually changed, the houses changed, the color and
smell and temperature of the air changed. Only the ocean remained the
same, sprawling its way from Hawaii on your left, squeezing the road
hard against the hills that dropped abruptly to the coast.

West of Topanga Canyon the rattletrap old beachhouses began, cheek
by jowl against one another. In these places the ocean seemed to disap-
pear until later, when the houses opened up, with maybe fifty feet between them, and you could catch an occasional glimpse of the water. The
mountains squeezed tighter where Sunset Boulevard comes in from
Pacific Palisades, and this constriction produced one of the paradoxes of
the trip, a feeling of opening up, as if you were looking down the narrow
end of a funnel to some eye-shattering brightness beyond. To think of it
this way you had to be going all the way out, to the open land on the
other side of town. If you were only going to have dinner at Alice's on
the pier or La Scala in the Cross Creek shopping plaza, you would never
reach the wide end of the funnel.

In the stretch where the beach shacks gave way to more formal
houses, there was once a place worth looking for. The house had a

verandah over the garage like a house in Hawaii might, and overhanging trees and two fan-backed chairs on the verandah. Next door there was a garden where bougainvillea bloomed around a small rectangle of green lawn. Together the house and the garden were authentic compared to the imitation New England cottages on either side, the mock English Tudors. Then one day whoever owned the house sold the garden lot and the new owners ripped out the palms and bougainvillea to build a dream house of their own. For a while the fan-backed chairs stayed on the verandah, then one day the chairs were gone. For a long time I mourned this loss. Sometimes now when I drive into the city, I look for that house and hope some new owner has restored it. But the paint job is cheap now and the whole thing is a mishmash.

When I drove out to Malibu in those days, dragging along the flotsam of my city life, I sometimes flipped the funnel and started from the wide end. When I thought of it this way, it was as if the trip itself had narrowed my options. Starting at the McClure Tunnel, where the Santa Monica Freeway becomes Pacific Coast Highway, the funnel's flow began its slow process of diminishing, reducing my hodgepodge of frustrations and the momentum by which they flowed from the wide end to the funnel's narrow stem. By the time I accelerated up the hill from the center of town onto the bluffland that was my final destination, only a few drops trickled out the funnel's end. Pure, the dross distilled, what remained were my expectations for the next few days. Although I never asked if anyone else had experienced something similar, I would have been surprised if most people didn't know something of this. This gradual dissolution from city to country was what going out to Malibu was about in those days. Reminders of the city faded as the things that rest the spirit took over. Yellow mustard carpeted the hills. The sky brightened and the air breathed cooler, smelling always of salt, sometimes of sage. The sun dropped behind the horizon in slow motion. "Aha," I would think to myself, "That is what it's about." Something like that was bound to happen, otherwise there wasn't much reason to make the trip.

It helped if you had a destination and a plan. Mine were essentially fixed. I went for sun and the early morning light. I went to ride a horse bareback down to the water, and for the smell of manure and eucalyptus trees on the salty air. I went to see the blaze of the late afternoon sun burn through Hana's picture window, and afterward the roundness of dusk, the anticipation of heading toward evening with nothing to do but just be.

I left the East Coast for California out of a small mill town in upstate New York. Summers we packed the family Plymouth full of suitcases and groceries and books and board games and drove two hours north to a lake in the Adirondack Mountains. A grateful nation had just elected General Dwight Eisenhower president, and in California the postwar boom was on. The last of the San Gabriel Valley's orange groves had already been torn out to make way for homes for returning GIs (a short twenty years before, Los Angeles had been the largest agricultural county in the state). East of Beverly Hills the house I would buy thirty years later had already been built, and the first of two families to live there before me had moved in.

I have fond memories of the summer we spent on that lake in the Adirondacks. I remember soft water and the scent of pine. I remember the heavy black spiders that scared my sister and me from our swimming hole, and jumping off the boathouse dock holding tight to my thick black inner tube. I remember toes stubbed on rocks, and splinters from skipping barefoot across docks. Shoes and socks soaked when I didn't watch where I put my feet in the wet Adirondack forest. My awareness of that natural world came mostly from my father. As a young man he had worked in a lumber camp in these same mountains, and the skills he taught my sister and me happened in the course of things, as we built a fire in the rock fireplace next to the lake or unhooked a bullhead from our fishing lines. My sister and I were no more conscious that we were learning something important than my father was that he was teaching us. My mother tried to instill in us an appreciation for more delicate things, but I applied her lessons also to the natural world, searching the forest for leaves and berries and bits of bark to weave into centerpieces for the dinner table. The physical world (I did not know it as the natural world back then), the world of straightforward cause and effect I discovered during those Adirondack summers, was the only world that mattered to me. My footprints in the earth were proof enough of my existence.

Sitting at Hana's table, I remembered these things. I remembered my sister sitting next to me in the middle seat of a blue-and-yellow rowboat, how we were allowed to use that boat because it was flat-bottomed, which my mother said made it safe. I remembered my sister and I rowing to the island in the middle of the lake alone in that boat, and how I disliked sitting in the front seat of the old red boat with the motor with my hands in my lap while my father figured out where we should go. "Let's go over there, Art," my mother would shout over the noise of the coughing motor, "let's see what that boathouse looks like." And my father would head the boat in that direction. Then he and my mother would argue about how much the boathouse cost and how much the boat probably cost.

My sister always gave up rowing when we got close to the island. She became the lookout. "Let's go this way," she'd point. "Or let's go back the way we came." She never told me what she wanted to see or why, and this made it easier for me to think.

After the rowboat, I paddled my canoe on that same lake, alone close to shore. I glided my smooth, thin-sided craft over submerged tree stumps and through quiet pools of lilies to see how far I could go before I ran out of water. My sister and I had been led to believe people no longer cared about this mountain world, that it was finished for the big lumber companies and the strip miners and the blue-stocking tourists, that it had been left to people like ourselves who could accept it on its own terms. On the car ride to the lake, we passed abandoned logging roads and the scars of gravel pits, the restaurants that had been left behind when the new road went in. What comfort, to know the way a place is now is the way it will always be.

Then one day a pile of *National Geographic* magazines appeared in our living room and challenged what my father knew. Wide-eyed at photographs of jagged peaks that mocked our worn-down Adirondack hills, in awe of grizzlies and of rattlesnakes fatter than copperheads, I set my sights on the West.

Sooner than I could have imagined, I was sitting in the first-class section of an American Airlines 707 flying low over San Diego. I had never been in so large an airplane before; I had never seen such an expanse of city lights. Twenty minutes later and my aunt and uncle and I are in a gray station wagon being driven down a narrow road overhung with tall, spindly trees. Fifteen minutes more and I am in a room in a small two-room bungalow on a hill in a town called Rancho Santa Fe, where the air is heavy with the scent of orange blossoms, and there are more of those spindly trees. Asleep under a thin blanket, I dream of the day I sat in the back of the school bus, in the very last seat against the back window, confiding to my best friend that I am going to California for two weeks and my mother had to get permission for me to take my homework with me. My friend nods, but I can see she's not impressed. I try to control my excitement. California!

The next day I have my first taste of avocado, soft and cool and green, and I learn that the tall, spindly trees, which are taller than any other tree I can see, with leaves that fall like a canopy—so that even outside I feel like I'm being sheltered—are eucalyptus from Australia. In the afternoon I swim in a pool shaded by more of these same trees, then join my aunt and uncle in the dining room, where all the chairs have arms and there are flowers I don't recognize on every table. Two nights later I am in Laguna Beach helping my uncle push a supermarket cart full of gin and vermouth and Cokes and potato chips across Pacific Coast Highway to the motel where we are staying *right on the beach*. At night I fall asleep listening to waves lap at the sand below my window.

In the morning my aunt and uncle and I board a bus for the trip up the coast to Los Angeles, where another of my mother's sisters will meet us. The hills we pass are round and soft and golden and there is nothing on them but a thin cover of wheat-colored grass. In Los Angeles my mother's other sister leads me two blocks from the bus station and points to a streetcar climbing a steep hill between a cluster of buildings: Angel's Flight. I don't know that what I am seeing is historic, that a decade later a flurry of redevelopment will sweep through downtown Los Angeles and a tunnel will be dug through the hill the streetcar tracks now climb. I have no way of knowing that when I return to southern California seven years later, the dreamy golden hills I saw out the bus window will be scarred with white stucco houses snaking row after row up the hillsides' seaward flanks. Or that a development of office buildings and department stores and specialty shops, a "Fashion Island" of steel and concrete, will rise just inland from Newport Beach, where once I saw a sleepy town of neat one-story buildings. I don't know that by the time I return to California, just as the old brick buildings and wooden houses west of downtown are about to be torn down and the area reassembled in a vision of glass and steel, Governor Pat Brown (known to believe that growth was California's destiny) will have pushed almost two billion dollars through the state legislature to bring water from the Feather and American rivers through the farmland of the Central Valley to homes in Los Angeles. I don't know three of the world's five largest dams have already been built in California, routing snowmelt from the northern mountains to water the dry south. I don't know that a sociologist named William White has already coined the phrase "urban sprawl" and applied it to Los Angeles.

Driving across the country toward Los Angeles seven years after the trip with my aunt and uncle, searching now for the golden land I remembered and still nurturing the vision I discovered in the pages of *National Geographic,* it never occurred to me that I was heading for a city, a bright glittering metropolis that would dominate its landscape like few others and be difficult to escape. I had never lived in a city before, and in the small towns where I had spent my life there was always a stretch of woods beyond the backyard, a river or pond down the street, always trees to climb and streams to ford, a stagnant summer pond that in winter would freeze and we could skate.

When I left the East Coast for California at the tail end of the 1960s, L.A. had not yet found its footing. There were still long swaths of green in the Hollywood Hills and ranches just over the crest in the San Fernando Valley. Northeast of the city, the steep, pine-covered mountains above Glendale and Pasadena suggested wilderness, perhaps adventure. A growing Hispanic community would soon be routed from its shantytown in Chavez Ravine east of downtown so the Brooklyn Dodgers could toss baseballs around, and when you ordered a hamburger in a cafeteria at the University of Southern California, as likely as not you would be answered in Spanish. South of the city near the harbor, the residential community of Palos Verdes had been laid out with bridle paths and horse fences, and in Santa Monica they still played polo on the field that once belonged to Will Rogers Jr.

I had no sense of how difficult it would be to move across the country from a small town to a city just beginning to feel its growing pains. My first trip east I wore boots and a long khaki skirt and carried saddlebags over my shoulder. As unsure of my identity as my adopted city, by my next trip back I was favoring jeans and western shirts and a bandanna tied with the v in front. I had no horse to throw saddlebags over, no hardscrabble ranch that required jeans and bandannas. I was teaching high school and taking night classes at USC. "Wait until you see the ranch," I told my niece the first year she visited from New Hampshire. Her eyes grew large until I was forced to admit there wasn't any ranch, not yet. But someday there would be. A California ranch, high in the desert, not one of those lush valley spreads you see in Colorado.

I didn't know what I was leaving when I left upstate New York for Los Angeles. Back then it didn't seem important that I could drive five minutes out of our worn-down mill town and see nothing but hayfields in the valleys and hillsides thick with maples. Or that in winter I could clamp on a pair of snowshoes and glide for miles along a broken fieldstone wall without seeing another person for the entire afternoon. "The West looks like the moon," my sister told me on the one visit she allowed herself. Back then, a thousand people a day were arriving in the Golden State, and the National Geographic Society had more members in California than in anywhere else in the nation.

In 1969, when my husband and I drove west across the country, newly married and hopeful for our new life, Los Angeles had the worst air pollution in the country. Radio stations kept track of air quality and warned when it was unsafe for children to "run, skip, or jump" outdoors. Almost ten years before, California had passed the nation's first law regulating automobile exhaust, but activists in an organization called Stamp Out Smog (SOS) were pushing for further controls (it would be another ten years, but members of SOS would help persuade Congress to set aside the Santa Monica Mountains from Hollywood to Malibu as an "airshed" for L.A.). The same year my husband and I abandoned the East, a spill from an offshore drilling platform fouled beaches in Santa Barbara and a citizens group called Get Oil Out (GOO) organized to have the oil platforms removed. Farther south, state traffic engineers were lobbying to build a freeway in the same mountains SOS was trying to save.

President John Kennedy was dead from an assassin's bullet, also his brother, Robert—on the kitchen floor in an L.A. hotel. An assassin had also felled civil rights leader Martin Luther King Jr. In Los Angeles, the African American community in Watts had turned its anger on itself, with thirty-four dead and a thousand injured after five days of violence. Up north a series of free speech demonstrations had raised havoc at the University of California's flagship campus at Berkeley, and in Washington the federal Supreme Court had stood firm in support of school integration, even if it meant busing children from one neighborhood to another. Everywhere hippies were flaunting postwar materialism, flirting with drugs in urban ghettos or running off to the country to live in communes. Across the world in Southeast Asia the United States was at war with Communist rebels in the former French colony of Vietnam. If one were inclined to drop out, as the language of the time put it— perhaps start a new life—the 1960s seemed the time.

By the time my husband and I drove through Iowa, past the Badlands of South Dakota and into Las Vegas, then across the Mojave Desert to L.A., the beachside community of Malibu had already embarked on its gradual transformation from a sometime resort to a permanent residential community. Reeves Templeman had left Topanga Canyon twenty years before to establish *The Malibu Times* next door to Las Flores Creek. The post office had long ago moved from the general store to the adobe plaza just inside the old Rindge Ranch boundary, and the Malibu Sea Lion was well established with tourists who motored out to Malibu on Sunday afternoons, took in the view, ate dinner, and drove home. Returning GI John Merrick had pushed farther west to Latigo Beach, where he financed a home with a ten-thousand-dollar government loan, met founding family sibling Ronald Rindge, and set to work building fiberglass canoes. By the time my husband and I moved into our rented townhouse in Culver City (clubhouse, swimming pool, and Jacuzzi), the number of people living full-time in Malibu had doubled, and John Merrick, now a municipal court judge, had already tossed a ceremonial shovelful of dirt to break ground for Los Angeles County's new office building near Malibu Creek. Beachfront property was going for fifteen thousand dollars a front foot.

About the time Merrick wielded his shovel in the groundbreaking ceremonies for Malibu's civic center, a young stockbroker from Pittsburgh named Harry Barovsky motored out to the beach one hot summer afternoon, liked what he saw, and found himself a place to live. A few years later Harry married Sharon Daly, a divorcée from Chicago with four children, and the two set up housekeeping on Las Flores Beach, settling into what passed for social life in the community. By local standards Carolyn Van Horn and Joan House, who like the Barovskys would play a role in local government, were late arrivals. Both women moved to Malibu with their families in the 1970s, just as my husband and I bought a house farther south, in Manhattan Beach. Both women were schoolteachers, Van Horn the daughter of a California Supreme Court judge and one of California's first women attorneys, House a veteran of the Peace Corps and pedagogy duty on a Navajo reservation. The Van Horn family settled on a lot on Point Dume, House and her husband on the beach just south of the Point.

Attorney Jeff Jennings, graduate of Venice High School, Yale University, and Stanford Law School, was among another wave of immigrants who struck out to Malibu in the 1970s, young professionals who were attracted by both the landscape and the lifestyle it suggested. A horseman, Jennings moved his family past the east-end beach neighborhoods to the open land in western Malibu and volunteered first for the Los Angeles County Beach Commission, then soccer and Little League, then as chair of the committee that would bring a high school to the community.

These leaders of Malibu's successful incorporation effort were not on hand twenty years earlier when the community made its first attempt to control its destiny, an embryonic effort that was rejected by 60 percent of the two thousand residents who went to the ballot box. John Merrick had run as a candidate for city government in 1964, but the judge actually disapproved of incorporation as a ploy to control development, as did publisher Reeves Templeman. Both men worried that cityhood organizers were kidding themselves. "After the war," said Merrick, "we were seeking peace and tranquility and to throw off city fetters. But maintaining the Malibu of the 1950s is impossible."

A similar declaration might have seemed appropriate almost a century earlier, when another city slicker struck out for Malibu's wide open spaces. In 1887 Frederick Hastings Rindge, orphaned son of a Boston wool merchant, turned his sights toward southern California as a place where a sickly man might regain his health. Ten years later when he took title to 13,000 undeveloped acres at the edge of the Santa Monica Mountains, Rindge might have envisioned a life for himself in the tradition of the old Mexican ranchos, but that way of life was fast fading. By the time Frederick Rindge left the East Coast to make his way west, California had been a state for fifty years, and Los Angeles had already developed a serviceable port at Wilmington, named after Wilmington, Delaware, the birthplace of its booster, Phineas T. Banning. As early as 1854—three years before Rindge was born—the Los Angeles County Board of Supervisors (perhaps already in a development frame of mind) had appropriated one thousand dollars to build a road to the dusty reaches of the San Fernando Valley.

By 1869 California was connected to the rest of the country via the transcontinental railroad's western terminus in San Francisco, and in less than ten years the Southern Pacific completed its trunk line between San

Francisco and Los Angeles. Swollen with tourists and hordes of hopeful settlers the railroads brought west, mid-nineteenth-century Los Angeles boomed from a sleepy, pre-statehood pueblo to a bustling community of fifteen thousand. Between 1887 and 1889, sixty new towns were laid out in southern California; had they all been built, they would have provided homes for two million refugees fleeing urbanization and bad weather in the East.

Rindge raised grain and ran cattle on his rancho in the manner of the old Spanish dons, shipping hides and beef to market from a private pier that still stands near the center of Malibu. Ranching, rather than farming, suited the rancho's rolling foothills, where water was sparse and its supply unreliable. Fresh water has always been hard to come by in Malibu. Wells sunk by early residents ran dry, and the "water problem," as old-timers like Louie Busch and Reeves Templeman like to describe it, wasn't solved until late in the 1960s when Los Angeles County stepped in to guarantee a regular supply. But the county had not planned well, and by the time I settled on Point Dume twenty years later, residents at the far end of a street could find their faucet dry if someone closer to the main line was having a party or decided to wash their car. Early settlers met the problem head-on, recycling their dishwater and the water from the rinse cycle of their washing machines on their gardens and leaving their lawns to go brown in summer—to the extent anyone had a lawn worth worrying about.

By the time I found myself wishing on the green hills above Malibu, the Rindge rancho was long gone, but the myth of Malibu's ranching legacy still held on at the far western edge of the community where the land was flat and still affordable, where there was still room for barns and horse corrals and nobody bothered about manure in the street or if a rooster disturbed the dawn quiet. Back then anyone who could afford it lived on the eastern end of the community closer to Santa Monica, where the commute to town was easier, leaving those who did the grunt work of the community, the plumbers and electricians, the old men who mowed weeds in summer, to settle Point Dume. East-end housewives might drive into Santa Monica to shop, but families on the Point drove north to the farm communities of Oxnard and Ventura to stand in line for their groceries with the stone-faced Mexicans who worked southern California's strawberry fields.

The table we gathered around at Hana's was oval, probably oak or mahogany, with all the leaves attached. If you took a seat near the head of the table, you looked into the living room at Hana's green velvet sofas and her heavy parchment lampshades—but if you sat at the opposite end, you had a view out the picture window to wide-open ocean and sky. We never ate at Hana's, so there were no salt and pepper shakers, no sugar bowl, and no candles, only a squat gray vase just large enough for a single flower in the center of the white lace tablecloth. When I think of Hana's table, I think of an even playing field: we were all equal when we gathered there. Tableau? Certainly. Some days it felt like a group of B-list players bent on their Broadway debut. Empty tableland, wide-open space you could stretch across. Giant scratch pad but never a scorecard.

I was an outsider at Hana's at first, the only regular who lived in the city and had a conventional job. One of the women who drank wine at Hana's cut hair in the shopping center up the street, and a county fireman slept in a camper next door and sometimes ate dinner with Hana, but I was the only one who got dressed up every day and went to an office. In any event it didn't matter how your accomplishments stacked up in the outside world, because taking your place at Hana's table required courage. You might drop by to talk with someone in particular, only to find a different crew minding the store—or you might amble over for some company and a glass of wine and run face-to-face into someone you hadn't seen lately who wanted a report on what you'd been up to. These were often the best moments, when you skated across the open space unprotected. We regulars were responsible for showing up often enough that there was always someone to talk to, but we were expected to prune our stories and not waste valuable table time.

Hana opened her house to us because, alone and with a family to raise, she had been where many of us still struggled. Once Hana gave you the nod and you took your place at the table, the rule was immediate and unconditioned acceptance. In her own exile as a refugee from the war in Europe, then as the divorced wife of an American GI—in her tolerance and her constant open house—Hana continued a tradition that dated back to the early days of the community, when "Judge" John L. Webster came to Malibu to die and, despite a lack of legal training, put in twenty years as the community's justice of the peace, or when Sgt. Peter McKeller completed his tour of duty at the Nike missile site at the top of Los Flores Canyon, drove down the mountain, and without a sideways glance bought the Union ·76 gas station near the old rancho gate. Or when actor Lee Marvin rode his motorcycle up to the bar at the Reel Inn and nobody blinked. Beneath the bedrock of the traditional residential community some Malibu residents aspired to, there ran a countervein that flaunted convention and was impatient with being told what to do.

We gossiped at Hana's table and swapped news—someone broke ground on the hillside lot one street over that everyone thought was unbuildable, a doctor from Brentwood just paid half a million for the blufftop acre that once belonged to Steve McQueen. Kate Franklin, a regular who lived across the street from Hana, was rushing to finish her kitchen before the county inspector drove by and noticed she'd done the job without permits (this was the game: save permit fees and skip the hassle of wrangling with the county). At Hana's table we worried about the number of out-of-towners we were beginning to see on the beach; we compared notes about riding trails we found blocked and complained about too many lights at night. I first learned about the sewer system the county had planned for the community at Hana's table and how people were organizing against it. We regulars took bets on how long it would take for the main line to reach Hana's neighborhood and how much it would cost to hook up.

"Did you flush?" Hana asked one evening when I sat back down at the table. I told her I always flushed.

"You shouldn't. Not if it's only wine." I raised an eyebrow. "We use septic tanks out here. If it's yellow, let it mellow. If it's brown, flush it down." Hana took a healthy drag on her cigarette.

"I see," I said, although I was barely aware of the difference between septic tanks and sewers. I left it that sewers were an artifact of cities and took septic tanks as evidence that my new friends in Malibu lived closer to the natural scheme of things.

I left the city at six o'clock on Friday evenings. An hour later, I was sitting at the table at Hana's, a glass of wine at my elbow; by nine the next morning I was on the back deck lacing up my running shoes. Down Birdview Avenue to the beach, past the old canvas-roofed restaurant that will become Splash and later Monroe's, I watch the early beachgoers spread blankets on the sand. Synapses fire, muscle cells kick in, and I lock my eyes onto the horizon between sand and sky. I remind myself to use the outside of my thighs: pull, don't push. I lean back, stomach in, spine straight.

In the city the special shoes come out, the funny thin shorts and the top with the mesh insert to keep my stomach cool. In the city, heat reflects off the asphalt pavement, and the air is oily with dirt and exhaust. Running in Malibu I breathe easier, not so much because the air is cleaner but because I am not hemmed in. Such modest circumstances set me humming; the gyroscope that has been tumbling off center all week starts to spin true. Back at Hana's I shower, pack up books and towel, and take the dog to the beach. Come afternoon I will shower again, this time on the back deck with the sea breeze prickling my skin. Then I will cook—hamburgers and a chocolate soufflé for whoever stops by—then pack books and dog and drive back to the city, where the gyroscope will slip back into its elliptical orbit, thudding hard against my ribcage like a washing machine trying to spin an out-of-balance load of clothes.

Alone in my house in the city, I wished on those Malibu weekends. I thought of the time I took my friend Colin Ingle out to meet Hana. He was younger than me, the son of a college dean, and Hana noticed his reserve immediately, then made it a point to call him "Ingle." I thought of the time Hana called, just back from Hawaii: "Come out for dinner. Bring your own steak." The friend I invited to go with me was insulted and bought steaks all around. I thought of the Christmas Hana insisted I celebrate at her house and the man I was dating wanted me home with him. I ate turkey and dressing and pickled cabbage at Hana's, then threw it all up in the gas station on my way back to the city. I thought especially of the nights we went down to the restaurant on the beach in our bare feet and ate Rigatoni Dudleys, then oysters and lamb curry. The sound of the surf bounced off the sandstone cliffs behind the restaurant. The cliffs smelled of sage.

I thought of riding a horse down to the beach with Hana's daughter. We rode saddle pads with no stirrups, she on her Arab mare, I on her old jumper. "Watch out," she shouted as I trotted toward the water. "He's going to roll." I came up on the other side of the horse grinning, my jeans stiff with sand and salt. I thought of sitting on the back patio with Hana and one of the table regulars watching Tom the turkey peck at stones at the far end of the backyard. Slowly, almost imperceptibly, the turkey began to move, thick black blob on long spindly legs. "He's headed our way," I warned the others.

"Tom's not a bad bird," said Hana, "too bad we'll have to feed him to the coyotes." She pronounced it coy-o-tees.

"He's coming right at me," I whined. For some reason, I was stuck to my seat. Tom straightened his course, corrected for drift, then, not stopping to check whether Hana or the woman sitting next to her might make better pickings, the turkey came straight at me, looked me in the eye, and pecked a hole in my jeans.

"Tom's not a bad bird," Hana said again, and I thought I saw her wink.

But why had old Tom picked me, and what kept me from leaping up and swatting the turkey away? Did one do such things? As if situations came boxed with instructions.

Alone in my house in Los Angeles, I remembered hearing a woman speak about what she called the earth's "deep structure," how the landscape frustrates our attempts when we try to rework it for human purpose because we consider only surface conditions: a house built in a floodplain will eventually be lost as a stream seeks its natural course; with the right jolt from an earthquake, a bridge built over fill will collapse. I wondered if the same effect might apply to people. The long, slow eat-ing away of nervous tension, the constant seesaw between who we are and what others think we should be, the wrong left turn off an unknown cliff, will it happen someday? Or like nature, does our basic structure exert itself, the framework that lies buried in the memories of where we have felt the most comfortable, the most who we are?

"I'd have to sell my house," I announced to the table one evening, late in my wine drinking. "And buy something out here." Hana lit a cigarette. Los Angeles County was on its third attempt to secure approval for a sewer system in Malibu, the National Park Service had just paid $45 million for 7,500 acres in the mountains in Malibu's backyard (none of us had noticed when, eight years before, Congress had voted to protect Malibu's mountains and sand as a national recreation area), and on Point Dume, entertainer Johnny Carson was building an estate above Westward Beach and had knocked down an entire cul-de-sac of houses to build a tennis court and outdoor play area.

"Why buy?" someone asked from across the table. "Bank the money and rent."

"What would you *do?*" It was Hana's daughter this time, pulling up a chair.

"I'd keep my job."

"And commute?" She said it like she couldn't imagine what that would be like.

"It would still be a new life."

Another night I sat alone at the table, a half-empty glass of wine in front of me while Hana fumbled in the kitchen making us something to eat. I heard cupboard doors opened and closed with a bang, the sharp clink of dishes set down on the tile counter. It was eight o'clock in the evening, and we had been drinking for three hours, just the two of us. Ordinarily there would have been five or six people more around the table, and Hana would be jumping up to bring more glasses or an ashtray, another bottle of wine. I had broken the pattern by driving out in the middle of the week.

"Maybe life needs a little tension," Hana shouted from the kitchen.

"You don't have any tension in your life."

"Me?" Hana plopped a piece of charred pizza on my plate, then pointed a finger backward at her chest.

"When I was young and I ran too far," I told her, "my legs ached from the knees down. My mother said I had shin splints, like I'd done something wrong."

"The muscle gets separated from the bone." Hana's voice was high and tight, like she was talking to a child about something they had been over too many times before. I watched her take a long draw on her cigarette, blow a cloud of smoke in the air, then grind the butt out on her plate. I reached for the wine, poured us each more. Pizza crumbs floated near the top of my glass.

"I have this dream that I'm standing on a ledge and no one knows where I am. The sun is hot and my legs are bloody from bushwhacking. But I'm outside. I'm in the open."

"Not me," said Hana, lighting another cigarette. She thumped the heel of her hand against the tablecloth. "This table is good enough for me."

When the time came, I rented an old ranch house one street away from Hana. Morning sunlight lazed through the front window, bounced off the kitchen table, then came around to lull the back of the house into easy twilight. There was a stone fireplace in the living room that I used for heat and a window in the shower I kept open most of the year. "Why out there?" a friend asked over dinner one evening in the city. "Nobody *lives* out there."

I told her I liked the sounds of horses. "And not having to wear shoes."

"Around horses?"

"No, inside the house. It's like being on vacation."

I shared my rented acre with an electrician who lived in a tool shed he had remodeled on the other side of the backyard fence and a surfer who bunked in an Airstream trailer on the other side of the electrician. My neighbor in the apartment beyond the breezeway in the main house was a sandy-haired bachelor who drove a faded MG and worked in the post office. I didn't have much to do with these other residents of my Malibu Cannery Row except to notice when the electrician's van turned left out of the driveway, most mornings just before I finished my first cup of coffee, or to be startled when the MG came down the road in the opposite direction from usual. My father dubbed my new digs the-house-that-Jack-built-and-the-Marx-Brothers-maintained and named the thug of a barn cat that came with the place "Lazarus" because the cat took his meals on the barn-shed roof and curtly refused all our offers of affection.

On a good day when the clouds are high, I can see a slice of ocean from my office window, down the draw that begins at the beach half a mile away. On good days the north wind pushes the fog inland and whitecaps rush toward shore. On Santa Ana days, when desert winds move the moist air out to sea, the horizon expands and the sea dwarfs the sky. I know what the ocean is like down there. I know how the waves break against the sand. I have seen gray whales off that beach and dolphins. I've watched shorebirds scoop in the wet sand for a meal. I have walked that beach in summer and winter, on bright fall days and cool days in spring. It is a common stretch of beach but enough to satisfy what I'm looking for, enough to remind me that my body is mostly the same salt water that crashes at my feet, and that I share the sloshing and pulling that keeps me breathing with the creatures I see before me and those who live in the waves.

I went to Malibu to take up residence at the narrow end of my funnel. From the perspective of Hana's table, I thought I saw the best of it, so well-defined that if I walked high enough in the mountains, I could see its bones showing. I wanted my life in Malibu to be suspended, broken loose of the city. I wanted to live where I could feel the effects of sun and wind and rain, where I could hear nature exert itself in the crazed cry of a coyote hunting a rabbit and the sharp *beep-beep* of a red-tailed hawk teaching her young to fly. It was a place to begin at least, one step back from sirens and windows sealed tight against soot, a step back from a postage-stamp yard and bars on the first floor. The life I envisioned in Malibu tingled and clanged in resonance, it thumped with an inner direction and rhythm, with the glow of a gaudy winter sunset and afterward the sky opening up like an upside down bowl of stars.

Pale ocean breezes wander off into the dusk and the enveloping fog. Blowing softly, anticipating where there might be hope. Pale breezes hoping the next twist of air will reveal a bright glistening sky instead of the harsh dust of pollution. Pale breezes pushing papers along the street, whirling at ankles, hoping for tomorrow, for a clean breath of air . . .

Blowin' Smoke

....

> A lot of people have built in harm's way.
> There's not enough access and not enough water.
>
> John Clement, former Malibu public works director

1993

From my bedroom window I see a pencil-thin glow on the ridge two miles north of where I'm standing, a flat line like the sun makes when it sets over a calm ocean. Above the red line a thick band of yellow bleeds into the dark sky, outlining the contour of the ridge as if someone has aimed a spotlight on the mountains from behind. Six o'clock on a fall evening and the desert heat wilts my lungs. Even without the light in the mountains, the acrid smell hanging thick on the night air tells me some-where, something is burning.

Myth has it that our neighborhood never burns. The foothills that drop toward the sea behind Point Dume fan onto a rolling plain, leaving no canyons for the wind to funnel a fire directly at us. The four lanes of Pacific Coast Highway that run along the Point's northern flank act as a firebreak and provide firefighters with a place to make a stand. Even so, the threat of a fire so close has some of us thinking about leaving. But where to go? All the roads are closed and our only way out is by water. The earnest young man at the television news desk tells us Coast Guard boats are stationed offshore, but for this fire-hardened community, rescue is not appealing.

"Beau Rivage," says my husband, meaning the restaurant ten minutes down the highway east of us. We are newly married and this is our first fire together. "Beau Rivage," says my husband again, and I nod, understanding that if the fire burns to the restaurant, I will leave.

"The dogs," he says.

"The beach," I answer, rummaging in the hall closet for a windbreaker and hat. If the fire burns to Beau Rivage, I will leave with the dogs for the beach.

We were caught between two fires that year, the Green Meadow fire, which had been burning to the northwest of Malibu for almost a week and accounted for the flames I saw from our bedroom window, and what the county fire department would eventually designate as the Old Topanga fire, not yet a day old but racing toward us at an urgent clip from the center of town.

The day the Old Topanga fire started in the hills east of Malibu, I was on the other side of the Santa Monica Mountains waiting at a roadblock for a highway patrol officer to check my driver's license to verify that I was a resident and not a looky-loo. Just as my turn in line came up, a dirty gray pickup pulling a horse trailer ran the red light on the other side of the highway and rolled to a stop. A heavyset blonde in muddy boots and dirty blue jeans jumped from behind the wheel. "I don't have any brakes," she screamed to no one in particular. "I don't have any brakes." The man in the car in front of her opened the driver's side door and walked slowly back toward the stalled truck and trailer. Three or four more pickups, each pulling horse trailers, stopped, then one by one pulled out around the blonde.

Feigning the pickup drivers' nonchalance, I put the Jeep in low and start up the hill toward home. Alone on my side of the highway, I watch a steady stream of trucks pulling horse trailers pass me in the opposite direction—a group of three first, then two more, then a fifth wheel pulling a six-horse trailer. The drivers take the steep turns long and slow, as if seeking reassurance in routine. I watch the blinking red of their brake lights gradually fade in my rearview mirror.

The line of horse trailers, the realization that I am the only one on my side of the highway, with only the whirl of my tires on asphalt to break the heavy silence, the fact that none of this is routine, puts me in mind of images from the final days of the Vietnam War, when TV cameras filmed helicopters plucking evacuees off Saigon roofs. In my case, the enemy is a fast-moving wall of flames.

Despite the empty road and the silence, despite the thud-thud-thud of the helicopters overhead, I am aware that in some part of my mind I am calculating whether I can make the appointment I've scheduled to get my hair cut in downtown Malibu. Only after I see sheriff's deputies stationed where the road I'm on dead-ends into Pacific Coast Highway and hear radio reports that all of downtown is under siege do I decide I should change my plans. Abandoning the excuse I've prepared for the sheriffs, who are now turning away even residents whose homes are in the path of the flames, I take a polite right turn away from the roadblock. Struck now by what's happening, I park the Jeep in the garage and walk directly to the television. I spend the rest of the evening watching Malibu burn.

It can be difficult to resist a crisis like a wildfire or a flood. Even as your rational mind attempts to assess danger and plan strategy, another part of you goes on red alert. You know immediately that you are being exposed to something out of the ordinary; perhaps you're being tested. How will you handle it? You don't want to become anxious too soon, because until a fire actually comes close, it is only a possibility. You smell the smoke and attempt to judge your distance from the flames. Ash floats like snowflakes in the air, dropping a thin gray film on the driveway, on the hood of your car, on the seats of the patio furniture. But if there is no smoke and no ashes, only the images on TV and the distant drone of the helicopters, what then? Do you stay or go? Without actually making a decision, I dig a cardboard box out of the garage, carry it upstairs to my office, and start to pack. But I am sloppy in what I select—my journals, an unfinished manuscript, one or two paperbacks—aware that I am not concentrating, that despite the TV images, I am not taking the situation seriously. Five years ago a friend threatened by a wildfire in Pacific Palisades rolled up his oriental carpets, threw them in the trunk of his Mercedes, and left. When I asked him how he could abandon a lifetime of possessions, he told me he'd just bought the carpets and they were all he could think to take. Like me, my friend was a newcomer to the urban-wildland frontier. Knowing such catastrophes only from TV, the fire wasn't real to him either.

"The carpets," I think to myself, "of course I'll take the carpets; they're family heirlooms." But what else? The battered teapot I've carried around for years? My grandmother's stew dish, now hatch-lined where the glaze is cracked, my aunt's raccoon coat? How do I assess a lifetime of possessions and assign priorities, how do I sift emotional value from practical worth? For God's sake the carpets and the silver tea service and the Waterford wine glasses and the raccoon coat. I laugh. I will need a van to haul it all.

Until a fire comes close, it is only a possibility, subject to the variables of fuel and wind and air temperature and what you hope is the competence of the firefighters. What you don't want to consider, perhaps aren't able to consider, is what happens if the fire defies the small odds working against it. Will your house be one that burns? Will you lose everything, the battered teapot, the raccoon coat? And can I imagine what it's like to lose everything? Standing in the kitchen, a cup of coffee halfway to my lips, my mind blanks. What would I take if I really had to go? I don't ask myself how I got into this situation. I don't ask, "What the hell are you doing here?"

Before I moved to Malibu, I thought of wildfires as occasional dramatic events. I watched from safe vantage points in the city as smoke blackened the sky over the Santa Monica Mountains. I called friends I thought might be in harm's way to let them know I was with them and to offer safe haven (and if I'm honest, to be in on the action). Although sympathetic, I never completely let the victims off the hook: if people would only do as they're told, replace their shake roofs and remove their overhanging decks, such devastation could be avoided. And damn the firefighters, by the way, for forcing able-bodied citizens from their homes.

The entire forty-six-mile length of the Santa Monica Mountains has burned at least once since official record-keeping began in the early 1900s.

The Woodland Hills fire in 1943 burned 15,300 acres; the 1949 Susana fire 19,080 acres; the Ventu fire in 1955, 12,638 acres; Sherwood-Newton, a year later, 37,537 acres, 120 homes destroyed and one person dead; the Wright fire in 1970 (one of the more costly blazes to char the mountains), over 30,000 acres, 403 homes and ten lives lost. Nor was this land empty. There were homes and schools, gas stations and supermarkets, clothing stores and designer yogurt parlors in the path of these flames, plus mule deer and coyotes and bobcats, even cougars. Ten plants listed as endangered are found within this fire-prone territory, which also hosts stands of rare California grassland (only 10 percent left statewide) and two excellent communities of valley oaks at the southernmost extension of their range. Fire has always been part of this mountain ecosystem, from natural lightning fires to the small fires Native Americans set to clear brush to our modern wildfires, ignited by a spark from an automobile muffler, a downed power line, or a disturbed individual with a match. Fueled by settlement, these modern fires burn hot. They plow wide swatches through vegetation and destroy habitat, leaving precious little to reseed.

Nineteen ninety-three was a bad year for wildfires in southern California. A fire in Sierra Madre in the hills above Pasadena preceded the fire in Malibu, as a fire in Laguna Beach had preceded Sierra Madre's blaze. The Old Topanga fire, which consumed some three hundred structures and killed three people, resulted in the largest contingent of firefighters ever assembled for a single incident in one day, not so much because the threatened area was so extensive (Oakland had lost three thousand homes two years before), but because of how houses can be squeezed into such tight quarters here. By the time I drove home at four o'clock the afternoon of the first day of the Old Topanga fire, flames had already burned up the northern flank of the mountains and down the other side and were jumping from rooftop to rooftop through the hillsides near downtown. By midnight, the eastern front of the fire was racing toward Pacific Palisades, and common wisdom had it if firefighters couldn't stop it there, the entire west side of Los Angeles was threatened.

Like most people, I have fallen prey to fire's images—the *spark* of an idea, *flames* of passion, enthusiasm *setting fire* to a thought. I have distant but solid memories of the fires my father set in the log lean-to on the shore of our Adirondack lake. I remember Girl Scout campfires I built myself, and fires in mountain cabins or on a beach. I have been warmed by these fires and cheered by their light and lulled asleep to their crackle. I know the hiss of a pine log added to a roaring bonfire, the snap of pitch exploding, the camaraderie of a campfire on a moonless night. I also know fire's renewal. The spring after the 1978 Kanan fire, I climbed from the beach up the mountains' western flank to where I knew there was a pond on top, ascending through lupine and poppies and fresh new growth on the manzanita bushes, the wildflowers so thick and bright against soil still dark with ash that it was like a Sunday stroll through a park.

We humans seem helpless in the face of a wildfire; the image is so strong it draws voyeurs and looky-loos. TV steps in as our surrogate, delivering catastrophe live and in prime time. I am ashamed now to admit that as the Old Topanga fire raged almost steps from my door, I sat and watched it on TV. As places I know and pass daily went up in smoke, I relied on images captured by news helicopters and edited in studios miles from the action. I can't kid myself as I did when Laguna Beach burned, that I am looking for news of friends in that community. My town is burning and I am getting it from the small screen where elements of tragedy are reduced to melodrama.

Turning away from the orange-red flames as they roar over a dark ridge near downtown Malibu, I wonder why it should matter if I watch the fire on television or go out and see for myself. What do I expect to discover that the professionals might miss? What is this feeling that I *should* be out there? Perhaps I don't like it that I have always accepted TV's version; maybe this time the firefighters won't stop it, maybe the wind won't shift. "VALIANT SURVIVORS," the headlines read. "RESIDENTS VOW TO MOVE BACK, REBUILD."

A wildfire is a TV news director's dream; a fire knocks even the game shows off the air because the story is BIG. But a good story requires a beginning, a middle, and a bang-up end—except on television, where the beginning suffices. Once the mop-up begins and the cameras shift, we forget the victims who for a brief moment were the focus of our attention. But what would it be like if the media finished the story? Would it be a classic struggle between a protagonist (residents in fire-prone areas) and an antagonist (the fire), which results in change (new ways of living on this urban-wildland frontier)? Hardly. In Malibu we thought of the fire as we might an enemy who had raped us; the way to fight back was to establish ourselves better than before. So it was that the minute the fire was out, we began to rework the encounter, acting as if the fire had been a fluke. Fire survivors petitioned the city council to increase the footprint of their new homes by as much as 20 percent, making their properties more competitive in the real estate market but bringing the roofs of their new houses closer together, a generous offering to the next fire. Lobbied by councilman Walt Keller, who knew what it was like to rebuild after a wildfire, our new government claimed sympathy with the victims' losses and waived building and permit fees, anticipating that the Federal Emergency Management Agency (FEMA) would reimburse the city's warmhearted gesture. News from the fire recovery effort in Laguna Beach and Sierra Madre suggested similar adrenaline-charged responses—the fires being an anomaly, none of us could imagine being called on to stretch our resources in the same way soon again.

The catastrophic images the media presents are not nearly as provocative as those who collect and distribute them believe them to be. The media images soothe actually, because they play to our preconceptions. In this world where illusion dominates, Malibu could bill itself the darling of disaster. "Come see our burned-out hillsides," as carloads of tourists did after the 1993 fire, when the charred hills looked like black-and-white photographs silk-screened against winter blue sea and sky. Malibu's perseverance makes good copy. Residents vow to stay, Caltrans crews clear Pacific Coast Highway and we're on our way again.

Or are we? I won't say the 1993 wildfire opened my eyes, but it did create a vague sense of unease. The fires always come at us the same way: up north-facing slopes, over the mountain crest, down through canyons to the sea. Three-quarters of the Santa Monica Mountains has burned at least once in the last fifty years. On average, some part of the mountains burns every year. Kanan Dume Canyon, at the western end of town north of my house on Point Dume, has been charred by seven major fires since 1935. Malibu Canyon, near the center of town, has burned six times; Topanga Canyon, to the south of us, has sustained four major blazes since the thirties. When you consider how fast a wildfire moves and realize that some of the fire companies called in to help can take a day to reach us, you begin to understand why when a wildfire burns in a populated area, there are bound to be losses.

During a fire, war images dominate. Women and children leave, men stay to do battle with the flames. Those who stick by their homes are the survivor elite, garden-hose commandos determined to accomplish what they believe firefighters can't or won't. Fire officials discourage such vigilantism. They want a clear field, no panicked traffic, no looky-loos, especially where turnaround room is tight. They want to be able to get their men out if the wind shifts or a hot spot flares. They want first crack at water. Still the stories circulate. A man stays to defend his home, and on either side of him houses burn. His wife won't hear until the next day that a helicopter saved him—a pilot on his last pass before dark who was startled to see a madman on the roof and made a final drop to scoop water from the ocean and drench the madman's house. Three years later the man's wife is still angry. Around her, neighbors lost everything.

Residents who lost homes in each of the three communities devastated by fires in that horrible year of flames organized to help each other through rebuilding. The publisher of *The Malibu Times,* who bought the newspaper from founding publisher Reeves Templeman six years before, lost his house to the fire. The newspaper became the fire survivors' newsletter, and I the Operation Recovery reporter. I researched information on city permits required for fire rebuilds, reported new building regulations adopted since incorporation and funneled press releases to the survivors from FEMA and the Governor's Office of Emergency Services. I passed on referrals to psychologists who specialized in trauma, sorted out information on filing insurance claims and purchasing new insurance, advised those who were caught in red tape how to protect their burned-out properties, then how to protect themselves from vandalism once construction supplies arrived and their new homes began to rise from the ashes. I interviewed an entrepreneur pushing the idea that Vietnam-era combat airplanes would make better firefighting aircraft than the cargo planes and Super Scoopers then in use, and the spokesman for a company marketing fire-retardant foam in containers that looked like scuba tanks, which he assured me had been used by the U.S. Army to protect mobile fuel depots and had seen service with municipal fire departments. At the suggestion of Councilwoman Carolyn Van Horn, I spoke with wranglers who rented goats to clear brush off hillsides. It seemed for a time that everyone had a solution to keep the devastation of 1993 from recurring. And if not a solution, then a reason it shouldn't have happened in the first place.

Drawn into the postfire recovery effort as a reporter, I began to develop a sense of what it is like to lose everything, and how this kind of loss can manifest itself. I listened to fire victims lambaste the Los Angeles County Fire Department for not having the small fire engines the U.S. Forest Service prefers, which the survivors insisted were better suited to the narrow hillsides where so many of Malibu's houses had been lost; for failing to provide out-of-town fire companies with local street maps; for not forcing absentee landlords to clear brush from their property; for protecting the homes of celebrities while others burned. One cool spring evening a year after the fire, I joined Operation Recovery members for their monthly meeting, where Los Angeles County fire officials were scheduled to answer questions about the department's postfire assessment and how recommendations that evolved from this effort would affect the community (since Malibu has neither a police nor fire department and contracts with Los Angeles County to provide both services, this means that decisions about firefighting policy and procedure are made thirty miles away in downtown Los Angeles).

After an exchange of pleasantries, the fire victims wasted no time letting their guests know they weren't happy with new regulations the department had adopted in the wake of the 1993 fire. What was this about property owners in remote areas having to reconfigure their driveways so fire engines would have enough room to turn around? Why no parking on streets in the burned-out parts of town? Why were residents required to install sprinklers *inside* their new homes? The five men sitting at the front of the room, coatless, in short-sleeved shirts and narrow black ties, answered the questions as they came, graciously disregarding the fact that all of this had already been explained in the newspaper. The new driveways were necessary because the county fire chief wanted to be sure he could get his engine out if the flames shifted. The parking ban on narrow hillside streets was to enable the department to implement its new policy of stationing engine teams at individual houses. The sprinklers were required because the water supply in many of the burned areas remained inadequate, and wetting down the inside of a structure would help protect against the spontaneous combustion common in wildfires.

As the firefighters wound down their presentation, the only fire survivor who had so far managed to rebuild asked flat-out what many other people in the room seemed to be thinking. "I want to know," she demanded of the polite men in the white shirts and narrow ties, "what you are going to do so this doesn't happen again." After a year, I had begun to appreciate the subtext that underlay the fire survivors' view of themselves. They saw themselves as victims of the fire, true, but also that they had been let down by those who were responsible for protecting them. But the firefighters know better: if the flames are hot enough and the wind is from the right direction, the fire is going to have its way.

One way Los Angeles County attempts to protect those of us who have settled in harm's way is to require that we establish a safe perimeter around our property. Current regulations call for clearing brush, trees, and other flammable vegetation within 150 feet of structures. The fire department has been less successful with suggestions about planting fire-resistant vegetation, and Malibu residents continue to use highly combustible eucalyptus and pine trees close to their houses and along property lines for privacy and as windbreaks. And while clearing brush may help protect neighborhoods, beyond Malibu's thin line of settlement, thousands of undeveloped acres unroll, some managed by the federal government, most by the state. Both the National Park Service and the California Department of Parks and Recreation have policies about the wild land they're responsible for in the Santa Monica Mountains. Russ Guiney, area superintendent for the California Department of Parks and Recreation, is understanding but firm. "The idea is to keep the land natural," says Guiney. "People who live near parkland have to remember that with the enjoyable part, there are also some risks." While many residents who live close to this wild land would like the agencies to clear what they think of as brush, Charlie Whitman, a prescribed burn technician for the National Park Service, insists a no-clearance policy is responsible management. All well and good, Whitman agrees, when asked about residents' concerns about fire, but removing the manzanita and toyon and wild lilac that grow in the mountains diminishes the value of parkland because it interferes with the manner in which the ecosystem functions. The intense wildfires associated with modern settlement are more efficient than the natural fires the plant communities in the mountains are adapted to. These modern fires carve wide swaths through vegetation, leaving the land bare and subject to erosion. Despite these concerns, both federal and state managers are required to clear their property within 200 feet of any private structures that existed before the agency took ownership. And no matter how much brush they clear, there is always someone who complains that they didn't do enough.

Federal and state land managers agree with Los Angeles County fire officials that the frequency and intensities of wildfires have increased as development has encroached on wild land. All of the major wildfires since 1925 have been human-derived, and both the number and size of fires have increased as the intervals between them have decreased. Driving north on Pacific Coast Highway a month after the 1993 Old Topanga fire, I slowed to allow five young doe to cross from their scorched feeding grounds to the marsh grass on the other side of the road. Returning home the same way a few hours later, I passed a Caltrans dump truck just lowering its rock plow to clear a deer carcass off the highway.

State senator Tom Hayden took issue with what he viewed as our community's propensity to deliberately place itself in harm's way, then look for handouts. Hayden coined the term "environmental selection" and said out loud what firefighters have long concluded: people should not be living here. Nature, said Hayden, should be the deciding factor in where we humans pitch our tents. Not a bad idea, except because the senator hadn't followed through and addressed the procedural questions this type of policy would provoke, it was difficult to take him seriously. Who appraises which areas are safe to inhabit (surely the flat, blufftop peninsula where I live would be considered acceptable)? Who develops the maps, enforces the designations, passes on appeals for exceptions? And how do we compensate those who already own property in these newly quarantined areas, not just for the loss of their physical structure but for what they came here for, their dream? Still, the underlying assumption has merit. Suffering could be alleviated and millions of dollars invested to more constructive purposes if people gave more thought to safety and less to their view.

A high pressure system forms over the desert. Winds push dry desert air westward over the inland mountains, where the warm air gains momentum for its final roar to the coast. Santa Ana winds blow, a spark ignites tinderbox vegetation, and houses burn. Does the wind, then, cause the fires, and do the fires cause the houses to burn? What if the houses weren't there? Are we brave to live where we do or simply shortsighted? One out of every seventeen people in this country lives an hour's drive from the mountains in Malibu's backyard. Any one of them could bring the spark that starts the next wildfire.

On Thanksgiving Day on the first anniversary of that terrible year of fires, I took a drive through the burned-out part of town. One or two houses had been rebuilt, but chimneys and concrete building pads were all that was left of most of the rest. In some places the land was so steep fireplace foundations rose thirty, forty feet in the air before the hearthstone and mantel appeared. I had never been in that part of town before. I had never seen the sweep of the coast from up there. I had never experienced the feeling of the ground dropping out from under the streets laid out like mountain switchbacks. Standing above the wide curve of Santa Monica Bay, I thought of the day I drove my father through the Hollywood Hills. Taken aback by the steep grades and the hairpin turns, he wondered who plowed those roads in winter. Then he remembered: out here we don't have winter, only fires and floods.

That Thanksgiving I started thinking seriously about the effects of a sixteen-thousand-acre wildfire, not just the burning, but what comes afterward. With the houses gone and the land bare, certain facts become difficult to ignore. In some places the burned landscape was so steep it required chain link fence to keep the rocks and soil from sliding. Erosion control experts call this rockfall netting, but it is actually long sheets of reinforced chain link laid end to end over the landscape, because without this twisted metal blanket the land would slide. In other places in the burned-out part of town, crews drove bulldozers and steam shovels into dry streambeds where they installed boulders to protect the banks from flash floods. Evil-looking metal cribs were laid across natural drainages to keep boulders and tree trunks from blocking highways, huge detention basins were dug to catch water, and truckload after truckload of hay bales were installed in vulnerable areas to help direct mud and debris away from roads and buildings.

Soil exposed to extreme heat develops a crust like the coating on a candied apple. While some of us in Malibu thought reseeding was logical to protect our barren hillsides, the fact is that any seed spread in the hope it might germinate and provide rainy-season cover can't penetrate this slick crust. When the rains do come, the seed slips off useless and the denuded hills slide, an effect that can last up to five years after a fire.

October 1996: Three years after the year of fires, with grass taking hold under the chain link and broken-up hay bales clogging our streams, I come downstairs for a cup of coffee on a Monday morning and find my husband sitting in front of the TV. I take a seat next to him and together we watch dirty gray smoke fill the screen. The wildfire that started two hours ago on the other side of the Santa Monica Mountains is still burning. The news people are calling it local, but at this time of year with a wildfire burning, there is no such thing as local.

"Maybe they'll put it out," I say to my husband as we watch flames skirt a subdivision. "Maybe they'll get it before it starts over the hill." But what is this other thought lurking in the back of my mind, this twinge of excitement at the idea the firefighters might not stop the blaze where it is, might never stop it? Is this what I want—for the fire to have its way just once, defeat the flying cranes that drag water buckets under their bellies, the C-130 cargo planes reconfigured to carry water or foam when the call comes, the firefighters' flame-resistant suits and reflective shelters, the helicopters and the water bombers and all of us who take this land for granted?

In another two hours, mutual aid companies will be filing into town. Six fire engines will be parked on the highway in front of Beau Rivage restaurant, the seal of the City of Beverly Hills shiny on one engine's lime green door. Monday is deadline day at the newspaper, but since electricity is already out in that part of town, I decide to deliver my copy to the office. As I point the truck east on Pacific Coast Highway toward the center of town, a steady stream of fire engines lumbers past me in the opposite direction—red and yellow and pale green trucks, their lights ablaze under the rusty pall of smoke that has dropped lower as the day passes. Fire engines are parked in the empty field across from city hall next to fading red water tankers and huge red bulldozers chained to flatbed trailers like caged animals. West of the field, someone in street clothes is directing traffic in front of the staging area, clearing the way for the engines to move out. Traffic in front of the civic center is bumper-to-bumper and I decide to forget the newspaper and station myself at city hall. Someone has set up a TV monitor outside the city manager's office and the local cable network is still broadcasting, but by the time a larger set is located, the screen has gone blank. If the cable company's assessment is accurate—that flames burned the cable and a switching station two miles down the highway from the civic center— the fire had already crested the mountains into Malibu before the incident commander had time to hold his first briefing.

Standing on the front steps of city hall, I watch fire chiefs in yellow jackets and pants and blue baseball caps with scrambled eggs on the brim crowd into the lobby. The firefighters greet each other warmly, shake hands and nod, then speak softly among themselves, like old friends catching up after a long hiatus. At three-forty-five, Jimmy Ryland, deputy fire chief from headquarters downtown, takes over from Malibu's local battalion chief and calls for a briefing in the city hall conference room. Stiff-legged, Ryland barks out his demands.

"Fuel trucks?"

"On the way, Chief!"—This from a sharp voice at the back of the room.

"Mechanics?"

"On the way!"—The same snappiness from another voice.

"Food trucks?"

"On the way."

"Who's paying for this?"

"Working on it, Chief."—Still another voice, this one less brisk.

In this room crowded with firefighters and representatives from the public agencies that manage the land over which the flames now rage, I sense the reality of the fire shift. Here the drama TV peddles is pushed aside in favor of strategies for managing the fire. At this point stopping the blaze is only a distant possibility. In these early hours of a wildfire, when it has gotten up a head of steam but has not yet fully declared its intentions, the goal is to protect objects of human value: officially, lives and property. Where the land fits in this equation is not clear. We residents experience the fire as crisis, but the firefighters think in terms of systems and procedures and hope this current encounter with the demon will be routine. A heavyset man from the county tries to pin down the fire chief about where he'll need water. The man from Waterworks 29 ticks off amounts available in storage tanks close to the path of the flames. "Tell me where you want the water, Chief, and I'll get it to you."

"I want it both places," Ryland snaps.

At four o'clock, I hitch a ride into the fire. Less than two miles from the staging area, flames are jumping twenty, thirty, fifty feet in the air on either side of the highway, generating smoke so dense it's like driving through a cocoon. As they did in the lobby at city hall, the firefighters here move slowly—a short, precise on-and-off with the hose nozzle to douse a burst of flames and conserve what they can of their water, a deliberate swing with an ax to remove debris. Amid great gusts of smoke that continually isolate one from another, amid flames bursting around them, the firefighters move hoses around casually as if they're out in their backyards checking for weeds.

On the far western front of the fire, Pacific Coast Highway is empty of traffic. Here and there groups of people stand by the side of the road peering in the direction I have just come from, shielding their eyes as if they're searching the horizon for an airplane that's overdue. At home on Point Dume, I find my husband with frayed nerves laying garden hoses along the foundation where there is easy access to the roof. Moving quickly, we stack what's left of half a cord of wood away from the stucco walls (aware we should have done this months ago) and back the Jeep out of the garage. Sheriff's deputies have already driven by twice, shouting through bullhorns that we should prepare to evacuate. I load both computers in the back of the truck, along with some handwritten notes I think are irreplaceable and some jewelry. Seasoned from the last go-around, I don't even consider the Waterford or the raccoon coat.

Up and down the street people pull out horse trailers and bridle stock. The man a few houses down with the new baby ties three motorcycles onto a trailer and hooks the trailer to his van. The homicide detective next door starts the old green pickup he keeps in his backyard and parks it in front of the house. Perhaps tonight the myth will be proved wrong; perhaps tonight the Point will burn.

Everyone is looking for news. Three years ago the cable channel was our lifeline to the outside world, all-news radio its backup. Tonight *Monday Night Football* has upstaged the fire's roughhousing. We call friends outside Malibu to hear what the TV is saying, but for people watching in Santa Monica or Costa Mesa, the difference between two canyons means nothing. For us, half a mile one way or the other is critical: should we stay or go? I again walk down the street. Four-wheel-drives and pickups stand ready in driveways; children's toys and TV sets are visible through the cars' rear windows. But the lights are on in all the houses. No one has left. A neighbor calls to tell us the fire is burning through Latigo Canyon, ten minutes east of us; horses were evacuated out of Winding Way an hour ago. Another neighbor calls to tell us her son is monitoring the flames by motorcycle from a fire road in the mountains. He tells her Winding Way is burning less than five minutes away from us and he's heading home to protect his own property. He tells her to pack.

At seven o'clock the next morning we wait still, not for the fire now, but for news of what we've lost. The wind has shifted, pushing the flames back on themselves (in the end it is always the wind that determines what burns and what doesn't), the sky is blue and bright over a calm ocean. We are at the beginning of another bright autumn day, except that the hillsides that were covered with chaparral yesterday are now black and bare. Fragile skeletons of oaks and manzanita are all that's left. I park the Jeep on a curve in the road above the burned area, where houses and barns stand out as islands of color in a sea of ash. Down the hill again, I stop to speak to a woman I know out for a postfire reconnaissance. Dressed in wool slacks and a sweater, her gray pageboy protected under a silk scarf, she looks like she's off for a round of bridge. "I had to wash my hair," she tells me. "It smelled so horribly of smoke." Nearby I see a fire engine tipped on its side. Later I will learn that a firefighter from Long Beach suffered a broken back when the engine slipped off the shoulder of this narrow road, and still later about firefighter William Jensen, one year from retirement, burned over 70 percent of his body. Before he is released from the hospital four months later, Jensen will undergo sixteen skin graft operations. These are the other dimensions of the fire's face.

Our second wildfire in three years cost over nine million dollars and inspired the usual round of debate about whether the money was well spent. When the local fire captain presented his report to the Malibu City Council, council members acknowledged how well the department's new policy of protecting individual structures had worked, but there were no questions about where the funds to pay for this defense were coming from. When Capt. Stephen Alexander moved on to brief a meeting of the community's emergency response study group, he had a rougher go. One volunteer wondered whether it wouldn't be less expensive to throw everything the department has at a fire where it starts instead of trying to control it once it gains momentum. But the fire chief admitted what firefighters knew from the get-go: even as they struggled to contain the flames where they started that Monday morning on the other side of the mountains, they knew the fire would burn to the coast. "We had everything we wanted," Captain Alexander told the audience. "We still couldn't stop it."

Such is the reality of life on the urban-wildland frontier, places like Malibu in northern California and Washington State, New Mexico and Colorado, where people live close to nature. If only there were a line between us and a wildfire as impermeable as an eight-lane freeway or a swollen western river. But that's not what the firefighters mean. They mean we're the line, the place where wild land and settlement meet.

I wanted to control my environment, the things about the city that bothered me. I thought the best way to accomplish this was to move to a place that seemed less besieged by what I found irritating, a place with less traffic, less hustle and bustle. My goal was not to be completely in the country, because that would be too far removed from what I knew, but far enough away so the city's influence wasn't dominant. Then right off I encounter a wildfire. Its rampage made me uncomfortable at first with the flames so close, but gradually I began to think I might accept the fire as a symbol of the progress I had made in escaping the urban world I suspected of leading me astray. A wildfire, after all, makes a mockery of what's manmade, the helicopters and the water bombers and television's efforts to keep track of the devastation. With the fire over and its damage contained, I did a little jig to congratulate myself on my capacity to live in this wild place—and how this gave me a leg up on the people I left behind.

But why had I wanted the fire to come? Because I wanted to see what happens, not the destruction so much as how a wildfire works, especially when people are trying to stop it? And whether my being here and the antsy feeling I get when the Santa Ana winds blow contribute to the fire's effect. You can't know all of this by watching a fire, but you can discover some of it. You can tell by the color of the smoke when a fire is burning through grass and when it's burning through chaparral. You can see how where people build a house or a barn or a tennis court plays into the threat. Perhaps what I really want to learn from a wildfire is not how I should live here—the impulse I originally thought drove me out to chase after the devastation—but why I chose this place. Perhaps I want to see this ability to coexist with such an out-of-control force as proof that something wild yet remains in me.

One day when I was walking the dogs in the mountains, a man in a pearl gray Mercedes pulled over to the side of the road and stopped me. "Those border collies?" he shouted out the window, and I nodded, noticing the freshly groomed black-and-white dog in his back seat. The man asked how I liked the dogs, and I told him they were fine as long as they had a job to do. He asked where the sheep were, and I told him about the co-op field across the freeway. Then somehow I got around to mentioning I lived in Malibu. Both the man and the woman in the front seat next to him perked up. "We live in Malibu," they said in unison, "up Encinal Canyon" (beneath the ridge I saw burning from my bedroom window). "You've got to be tough to live in Malibu."

I looked at the shiny dog leaning against the leather in the back of the Mercedes, then at my two dogs, who hadn't had a bath in a year except for the water tub at the sheep field. I wondered what this guy would do with an everyday, persistent thing like snow instead of a once-in-a-while big occasion like a wildfire. Would he think he was such hot stuff then?

Cowboys and Indians
. . . .

A DRAMA IN THREE ACTS

1994

ACT ONE, IN WHICH THE REPORTER IS INTRODUCED TO THE
STORY AND THE PLAYERS:

JACK SKENE in the role of the Mortgage Broker

PAUL VARELA as the Director of the Chumash Cultural Center

DR. KOTE LOTAH as The Traditionalist

A-LUL'KOY LOTAH as Medicine Woman

DR. CHESTER KING as the City Archeologist

QUN-TAN SHUP as Medicine Woman's son and Malibu's
    Chumash Manager

ERNESTINE YGNACIO-DESOTO as the Descendant of the Last
    Chumash Speaker

I am in a bubble, suspended above normal space and time, lost in the still
frame of a moment that could last forever. The harsh October sun burns
like sandpaper against my skin as the hot desert air pushes the last fila-
ments of moisture westward, even here on this island twenty miles off
the coast. The shadowed deep green of late-season oaks marks a horizon
with the pale afternoon sky in which the sun will soon drop like a stone,
turning everything in sight a crass vermilion. I know instantly the appeal

of unpeopled places, their release from human reference. I float here, citizen of nowhere, dependent only on random configurations of sun, wind and air, chance assignations that bear no stamp of accumulated time and are independent of the arbitrary demarcations of the human calendar. Here I am free to dream, backward into history or forward to wherever my arrogance might prod.

Today as most days, I choose the past, going back only as far as I have been thinking lately, to this island before roads and the steamship pier, before the summer cottages that fan out from the beach. I wonder what it would be like to walk this land instead of bouncing along its surface in a rattling jeep, to know its depth and shadow. To sleep always with wind on my face and eat mashed acorns that taste of the soil. Relics of the people who slept under blankets of fog and walked trails just wide enough to put one foot in front of the other lie hidden beneath me, bits and pieces of a culture their modern descendants know mostly by rumor. My bones ache with empathy for the timelessness in which these lives were suspended, unencumbered by our modern determination to mold place to our human will and our futile efforts to bend time around the angles of our demands.

On the mainland I don't think such thoughts—the hand of man is too heavy on the place—but I do not begrudge others the chance to search in the soil for clues to their ancestry. I have only recently come to understand that to know their religion and culture, the modern descendants of the Gabrielinos and Chumash who once lived on this island and on the mainland close by must hunt among the garbage heaps and burial grounds of those who went before. I believe I am behind them all the way, their gods bless them for what they find.

Why is it, then, that I find myself sympathizing with the young dark-haired Mortgage Broker sitting with his family in the front row of Los Angeles County Superior Court? Why am I not more sympathetic to members of the American Indian Movement who are challenging this man's bid to build a house on property they say may contain important clues to the heritage of Malibu's Native Americans? How is it I find merit in the proposal being put forward by our city attorney, which flies in

the face of what our city archeologist has recommended to preserve artifacts that might be found on the Mortgage Broker's property? Why have
I chosen to overlook that this man, sitting with his wife and two young
sons in the front of the courtroom, plans to build an eleven-thousand-
square-foot house on five acres of undisturbed blufftop land? An eleven-
thousand-square-foot house plus a six-hundred-square-foot guesthouse,
a monster estate that will vanquish its natural setting. Why am I not more
frustrated that the judge appears to be insensitive to AIM's claims?

Half the courtroom back from the Mortgage Broker and his family,
a tall, heavyset man in a paisley shirt with shells around his neck sits
next to an older woman dressed in street clothes. Farther back a group of
men and women struggle to find seats. One of the women wears a headdress of eagle feathers, and the man next to her carries a drum. The
man in the paisley shirt is the Director of the Chumash Cultural Center
(twenty minutes over the Santa Monica Mountains north of Malibu).
The woman in street clothes is a descendant of the Last Chumash Speaker. Both are in court today to support our town's proposal to protect whatever Native American artifacts might be found on the Mortgage Broker's
property. Although most of the men and women at the back of the room
are also Chumash, they are at odds with the director of the Chumash
center and the woman with him. The short-haired woman dressed in
black sitting with the Chumash at the back of the courtroom is a leader
of the local chapter of AIM, the trim blonde standing in front of the
judge is AIM's attorney.

The judge tells AIM's representatives that instead of this lawsuit, they
might better have invested their resources in a scholar who would investigate the Mortgage Broker's property. The judge reasons that if the
site is as important as AIM claims, any number of qualified archeologists
should be interested. She admonishes the lawyers on both sides that this
is a case that should have been settled out of court.

As the legal banter wears on, I wonder what makes one case a case to
settle and another not. Who among those assembled would have to abandon their dreams? Would the Mortgage Broker have to give up living in
grand style overlooking the Pacific? Might AIM have to settle for some-

thing less than striking a definitive blow for Native American rights? Sitting in court today, it strikes me they all might lose. The law is inhospitable to dreams and intolerant of emotion. The law brooks little consort with the ambiguity that permeates most human relationships. The law defines its terms in black and white, in verdicts that become arbiters of other people's dreams. Most of all, a legal opinion suggests virtue of the winner and questionable behavior on the part of the loser, which is what makes taking a matter to court so seductive. We are handed not only a decision but also a value judgment: *They* are wrong and *we* are right.

We are assembled in court today, waiting for the judge to hear the attorneys' arguments, because Malibu's city archeologist believes the parcel of land on which the Mortgage Broker wants to build his estate contains a section of the undisturbed Native American village of Sumo, which once stretched from the foothills of the Santa Monica Mountains to the sea. I wonder how he can be so sure, since other experts I've spoken with tell me you can't determine the value of a site until you dig.

There were no Chumash on Santa Catalina Island. The island natives called themselves Pimugnans, descendants of Shoshone-speaking tribes who migrated into California from the east. Although Gabrielinos also settled on the mainland at what is now Los Angeles, archeologists consider the island Gabrielinos more advanced, in part because they were influenced by Chumash from the islands off the coast of what is now Santa Barbara. The interaction between the two groups eventually obscured differences, leading some investigators to describe an advanced Cataliño culture known for its superior craftsmanship in bone, shell, and stone. Unfortunately for their descendants, Natives from both island groups were conscripted into the Franciscan missions. The last Pimugnans were removed from Santa Catalina Island to Mission San Gabriel east of Los Angeles, and the Chumash gathered into settlements at Ventura and Santa Barbara.

The Franciscans baptized just over 53,000 adult Native Americans and buried over 37,000. At no mission did the number of births ever equal the number of deaths. But the Indians fared no better after the *Americanos* took over. Because Natives were not granted citizenship when California was admitted as a state and therefore could not own property, they were at the mercy of the Anglo invaders, who appropriated their land for livestock, robbing them both of their way of life and the source of their spiritual well-being. Four years before statehood, California had 72,000 Native Americans and only 5,000 white settlers. In only fifteen years of Anglo control, the state's Natives were reduced by more than two-thirds.

The Europeans who preceded the Americans in southern California found the Chumash living in isolated pockets from San Luis Obispo, above Santa Barbara, south to what is now Malibu, and today these settlements provide a loose geographical rationale for modern Chumash clans. Although the Santa Ynez band northeast of Santa Barbara are the only officially designated Chumash, this hasn't deterred members of the Owl Clan living south near Ventura from claiming they represent what remains of the once-flourishing coastal bands. This situation of contradicting allegiances is complicated by generations of intermarriage, which has further diluted the remnants of Native American cultural and spiritual mores that survived the missions.

When I began researching the Gabrielinos on Santa Catalina Island, I was startled by the incompleteness of the information and the fact that there appeared to be no living descendants who might provide firsthand insight into their culture. But what would I have asked if I had located a modern Gabrielino? Tell me stories of the island that will make my research real? Tell me what it is like to be a Native American in an Anglo culture? Tell me what your issues are?

They handed me the story like a hot potato, but not without the suggestion that it involved feuding Chumash families, one group aligned with the Director of the Chumash Cultural Center and the other associated with a leader of the Owl Clan who identified himself as a Native American traditionalist and earned his living monitoring commercial and residential construction to protect artifacts that might be present.

When a story emerges out of nowhere like this, it means beginning with the present and moving backward. You know that somewhere there will be a victim but worry that whoever this might be will lack what you most want to establish, which is a sense of the larger situation. Victims are prone to ramble, beginning their accounts at the conclusion, on the premise that the freshest insult is the most telling. Villains take a more circuitous route. "You know how things are," a villain will confide, as if the two of you are on the same side.

I called the Director of the Chumash Cultural Center first. From what I could see, it appeared he might be the injured party. Before I could ask my first question, the man I had selected as my probable victim launched into a discussion of the Native American Heritage Commission's Most Likely Descendants List, an official record of California's Native Americans. When I wondered what this had to do with the story I was chasing, the Director of the Chumash Center explained that a member of the Owl Clan—the man I would come to know as The Traditionalist—had recently put the commission on notice that he represents the whole of southern California Chumash, including the Director's clan. Since this Owl Clan activist has yet to verify his Chumash ancestry through either of the two conventional sources—records from the missions or from the Bureau of Indian Affairs—the Director of the Chumash Center is insulted. And fighting mad.

A spokesperson for the commission explains that Native Americans such as The Traditionalist who work as monitors on construction sites have the authority to call for job shutdowns if they believe artifacts or remains at the site might be lost or damaged. He tells me the Most Likely Descendants List is valuable because communities like ours use it to locate Natives to employ as monitors.

And the man who thinks of himself a traditionalist—is he on the list?

Not if he can't document his heritage.

Not even if he was one of the first to step forward when the state passed its cultural resources legislation over twenty years ago and has earned his living as a monitor ever since?

Not if he can't document his heritage.

City councilman John Harlow, known around town as the community's property rights advocate, calls to alert me to other victims: homeowners and businesses the councilman insists have been forced to pay too much for the services of Owl Clan monitors. Harlow confides that Los Angeles County paid more than $100,000 for monitors during the installation of ten miles of new water mains on Point Dume, and the Mortgage Broker is facing a $46,000 bid from The Traditionalist to monitor excavation during construction of his estate. The councilman further suggests that the Mortgage Broker's decision to consult the Director of the Chumash Center for a second opinion has produced a major glitch in business-as-usual for The Traditionalist, who until now has enjoyed a monopoly on the monitoring business in Malibu, benefitting handsomely from his assessment that property owners are willing to pay extra for the timely delivery of an archeological permit.

That Malibu is rich in archeological resources is well established. At least a thousand Chumash sites have been documented in the Santa Monica Mountains, one of the densest collections of archeological resources in any mountain range in the world. The Chumash found fresh water and food at the mouth of Malibu Canyon, where Frederick Hastings Rindge would later establish his ranch headquarters, and rolling blufflands like the Mortgage Broker's were favorite village locations. The man who is now employed as Malibu's official archeologist discovered the site on what is now the Mortgage Broker's property thirty years ago, and although he insists the village is so large that only part of it is contained on the property, this find remained untouched by pick and shovel until the Mortgage Broker's plans triggered an investigation. Although what actually might be discovered remains vague, the City Archeologist's preliminary estimate is that the scope of the required investigation and measures to protect what's found could set the Mortgage Broker back as much as $300,000.

The Mortgage Broker tells me he doesn't consider himself a victim. Yes, he knows his property may contain a Native American site. Yes, he has met with the City Archeologist and is prepared to abide by the suggestion that he move his house and perhaps even construct the building on pylons. After all, his wife is one-sixteenth Cherokee. Likewise, he has arranged to donate any artifacts that might be found to the Chumash Cultural Center and to make arrangements for reburial of any human remains. He is concerned, however, about The Traditionalist's monitoring bid.

. . . . .

ACT TWO, IN WHICH THE REPORTER IDENTIFIES THE
DYNAMICS OF THE STORY AND ASSESSES THE STAKES AS
VIEWED BY THE PARTICIPANTS.

By provision of Malibu's cultural resources ordinance, one of the first laws to be adopted by the city council on the heels of incorporation, all new construction must be submitted to the archeological archives at UCLA for a twenty-five-dollar "quick check" to flag property likely to contain Native American resources. The archive employee who handles these requests happens to be married to the City Archeologist, and if her research determines the property in question does indeed contain resources of archeological importance, her husband is empowered to require a preliminary study to determine the extent and possible quality of whatever artifacts or remains are present. If the resources are found to be significant, more-detailed studies may be called for as a basis for specifying mitigation measures to protect what's there.

Day One, the first week of investigation: The Traditionalist is not home when I telephone, but his wife, Medicine Woman, is happy to speak with me and impress me with her sophistication in the Anglo way of doing things, tossing off legal terms I have to research. Medicine Woman insists we residents of Malibu are being cavalier about resources that are important to her heritage. She commends her husband and the City Archeologist for their efforts on behalf of Native American culture. When I ask how she feels about the Director of the Chumash Cultural Center and his competing bid to monitor construction on the Mortgage Broker's property, Medicine Woman tells me it's disappointing that Natives who have been persecuted for so long can't get along.

And the Mortgage Broker?

"Whatever happens to the mortgage broker," says Medicine Woman, "he's got it coming."

The City Archeologist is delighted to speak with me. He is proud of Malibu's policy of protecting its Native American heritage. He complains about the shortsightedness of his critics. He is honored to be joined by The Traditionalist and his stepson (now serving as Malibu's Chumash Manager) in upholding the community's commitment to Native American rights. He faxes fourteen pages of his résumé.

Day Two: The Mortgage Broker tells me that discovering Malibu has changed his life: "Never has a place so captured my soul." He recalls the day he discovered his land might be valuable to Native Americans: "As we walked along, the city archeologist picked up an occasional shell or broken rock, which he identified as artifacts. I was worried beyond belief about having to spend money I didn't have."

Day Three: The Director of the Chumash Cultural Center calls to up the stakes. He tells me not only that The Traditionalist can't document his Chumash heritage, but that an anthropologist at a noted local museum has traced his maternal ancestors to Baja, Mexico, far south of where the Chumash are known to have settled. I verify the information, then telephone The Traditionalist for a reaction. But the man who by now is on my list of probable villains deftly skews this liability to his advantage, explaining that because his parents escaped the Franciscans, they were among the few Natives who were able to safeguard the old ways. "Mission Indians," The Traditionalist sneers at the Director of the Chumash Cultural Center and his followers, who must make do with whatever scraps of religion and culture survived the Franciscan padres.

Day Four: A woman who teaches anthropology at a local university telephones to tell me she is perplexed by how Malibu is administering its cultural resources ordinance. She repeats Councilman Harlow's complaints about the Owl Clan's fees and insists she supports protecting Native American artifacts but fears the town's policies may spark a backlash. She tells me the site on the Mortgage Broker's property may not be Chumash; in fact she believes it's Milling Stone Culture (which I recall from Catalina Island is an earlier, much less developed civilization), and therefore whatever artifacts might be present are not as valuable as the City Archeologist insists. I ask if Medicine Woman is correct when she refers to the site as sacred because it's old. The anthropology teacher tells me "sacred" is a designation that can only be applied to places used for religious purposes.

Day Five: I pause to take stock. That there is at least potential for conflict of interest in the arrangement The Traditionalist and others of the Owl Clan have established with the City Archeologist seems clear. Both The Traditionalist and his wife were involved in drafting the ordinance specifying that Malibu's Chumash Manager should confer with the City Archeologist on construction that requires the services of a Native American monitor. I also establish that monitors other than members of the Owl Clan stand ready to work in Malibu, including the Director of the Chumash Cultural Center and his clan, as well as the Santa Ynez tribal council, whose members charge twelve dollars less an hour than Owl Clan monitors. There is also the fact that although a municipal employee, the City Archeologist has been engaged by residents to conduct investigations he and the Chumash Manager have called for. Finally, there is the City Archeologist's wife. In her position at UCLA she has access to a wide-ranging database on Native American sites and the extent to which each has been investigated. Although this information might be helpful if it were made available to property owners, if the City Archeologist shares it exclusively with The Traditionalist and his clan, even in a casual way, it would seem to give them a leg up in soliciting business.

That The Traditionalist has tainted the work of Native American monitors is clear to the Director of the Chumash Culture Center and his ally, the Descendant of the Last Chumash Speaker, who have charged the Owl Clan with overstepping its bounds and using less than ethical tactics to squeeze a regular cash flow from work they consider should be undertaken by volunteers. "Take the money out of it," the Descendant of the Last Chumash Speaker tells the Malibu City Council. "You'll never solve this problem until you take the money out of it."

For years on Halloween I chose an Indian costume, a child's version of Native American I assembled from picture books and what I saw in the movies—mostly Great Plains Indian—fringed dress, long feathered headdress, knife at the waist. Like most children, we played cowboys and Indians, and equipped with my costume, I typically chose the Indian side. Likewise, given a choice at Thanksgiving between a gray cardboard Pilgrim's hat (difficult and time-consuming to assemble) and a paper band of colored feathers, I always chose the feathers. The Pilgrims were all but done in when they landed at Provincetown and stole a cache of the Natives' corn. Soft-peddling the transgression, the Indians saved the colonists from starving when they demonstrated their trick of using anchovies as fertilizer. As a child I wondered what prompted the Indians to aid the strange people who dressed and spoke so differently from themselves. I wondered what in the Natives' experience made them identify with the Pilgrims' plight.

I was ten when I exchanged my squaw dress for a hobo costume at Halloween, and I wasn't much older, I'm sure, when I began thinking Natives in this country had been given a raw deal, that instead of reciprocating their inclination to join up and lend a hand, we Anglos had elected to emphasize our differences. I wondered why, if there were so many more of us and we were so superior in skills, we didn't take better care of these people who had made it possible for our ancestors to survive in an unknown landscape. But it wasn't until I was researching the Gabrielinos on Santa Catalina Island that the idea of Native Americans finally became real to me: They were women in tulle skirts and seashell necklaces who carved smooth soapstone bowls and gathered acorns to cook in tightly woven baskets. They were shamans who ate jimson weed and had extravagant visions.

In Malibu, I began to fear that in dispensing my good wishes toward Natives, I might have in fact thrown up a wall between myself and these people I professed to honor—*they* the conquered, *I* a member of the subjugating culture. I wondered if my current ambivalence in the Mortgage Broker's case might be related to what the mounting evidence suggested, that our community's cultural resources ordinance was doing more harm than good among the Natives we professed to aid. Unlike the state's environmental protection legislation, on the books for almost twenty years before Malibu passed its own ordinance, our local regulations didn't specify a limit on what residents could be required to pay when Native American resources were discovered on their property, nor did it make provision for the town to help bear the expense of investigating and protecting those resources, especially in such extravagant cases as the Mortgage Broker's appeared to be. As I had sympathized with Los Angeles County firefighters when they were taken to task by victims of the 1993 wildfire, I again found myself gravitating toward the less correct side of the argument, this time identifying with an individual whose actions I would normally have disdained. An eleven-thousand-square-foot house on five acres of undisturbed blufftop land, plus an extra six hundred square feet for guests!

■ ■ ■ ■ ■

ACT THREE, IN WHICH THE PLOT THICKENS BUT
LITTLE IS RESOLVED.

Malibu's mayor, an one-term council member allied with antidevelopment activists, insists he sees no conflict of interest in the fact that the City Archeologist gets paid for doing the studies he calls for, or that The Traditionalist shows up on digs his stepson has an inside track on. Driving home from the interview, I stop to watch a Native American in blue jeans and a plaid shirt sitting on a campstool reading a newspaper. Directly in front of where the Native sits shaded under a eucalyptus tree, a utility crew is digging a trench for a new water line. I wonder by what instinct or procedure this Native American monitor knows when to check the ditch in front of him for beads or a piece of bone.

When I ask Councilwoman Carolyn Van Horn, who has been vociferous in her support of Malibu's cultural resources protection policies, the same questions as the mayor, she brushes me off. What's this concern about conflict of interest when the rights of Native Americans have been neglected for so long? But it's not long before my reporting and the Mortgage Broker's protests open a door, and more residents come forward to lodge complaints about lengthy work stoppages and extravagant monitoring fees. Bolstered by his file of correspondence, the city manager suggests the city council consider revising our law. Reluctantly the mayor names a subcommittee. Their finger in the wind, the Native Americans who developed the original ordinance also commit to a revision, but their effort flounders when meetings are canceled because the task force can't raise a quorum to vote. I begin to sense the story entering another stage: it is no longer "developing." It has become "mature."

Incident One: I attend the dedication of the Chumash Cultural Center. Under a grove of oak trees, I watch gray-toothed elders, regal in their folding lawn chairs, receive the deference that is their due. I photograph Native American dancers and children who listen eagerly as their mothers explain what they know of the dance. I meet scholars and archeologists the director of the center has recruited to support his efforts.

Incident Two: As the city council's subcommittee considers checks and balances that might be included in a revised ordinance, Native Americans on both sides, those who support the Director of the Chumash Cultural Center and those in The Traditionalist's camp, begin attending city council meetings. The City Archeologist appears with a band of Chumash who favor The Traditionalist and place a hex on council members. Afterward, he dances in celebration with the Natives, his unbound hair flying.

Incident Three: When I call to check on a development in the story, the City Archeologist dresses me down, charging *The Malibu Times* with being a puppet of developers. A check of the paper's back issues establishes that the Mortgage Broker once advertised in our pages.

Incident Four: A retired actor whose son is the chairman of the task force that developed Malibu's original cultural resources ordinance appears before the city council to urge continued protection of Native American sites.

Incident Five: Despite the turmoil and all the ink the newspaper has invested in the story, The Traditionalist is selected by a local school to speak about his Chumash heritage, a not-so-illogical choice since he and Medicine Woman have long been Malibu's most visible Indians. The Director of the Chumash Center is hopping mad.

Incident Six: After months of petitioning for redress, the Mortgage Broker files a two-and-a-half-million-dollar lawsuit against Malibu.

Incident Seven (the action that turns the corner on the story): The city attorney calls to tell me she has taken matters into her own hands and has proposed a settlement with the Mortgage Broker. The local chapter of AIM immediately objects and announces it will file an injunction prohibiting any further construction on the Mortgage Broker's property. Almost as quickly, the executive director of the state office of AIM telephones to discredit local chapter leaders, claiming they have not been authorized to take a position in this case.

My file on the story now bulges beyond its original manila folder into a thick looseleaf notebook in which I have collected copies of The Traditionalist's bid on monitoring the Mortgage Broker's property and of documents relating to the City Archeologist's investigation of other Native American sites in Malibu. I have copies of Medicine Woman's genealogy as well as her son's, numerous letters to the city from an ever more exasperated Mortgage Broker, some in flamboyant and almost unreadable handwriting, and the city manager's measured responses. I have notes from my conversation with the former city archeologist in a town to the south of us, who tells me it's inappropriate for our city archeologist to work for residents while he's on staff, and more notes from my interview with an archeologist the Mortgage Broker hired for a second opinion, who tells me Malibu is too hot to handle and he's not interested in getting involved any further. Once again, I pause to take stock. Sacred versus rare. Legal right versus moral obligation. Persecution versus negligence. Enlightened concern versus the law. What was the rush to pass a local ordinance when a state law already existed? Had Malibu consulted with other communities about their cultural resources policies? Had we inquired about the pitfalls associated with administering this kind of ordinance?

More questions: Am I sworn to report only what appears to be true on the face of events, or might my job be to offer perspective on the contents of my bulging files, the anguish, the hurt feelings, the fractured dreams layered within their pages? If I go further and unravel each individual player's knotted line of experience, will the real dynamics of the story reveal themselves? And would this be like cracking open a nut to discover hidden fruit or more like peeling an onion where, layer after layer, there is only more of the same? What happens when a public figure can't see past his fear or her anger or when a person who would lead is unable to neutralize a grudge? Are we naïve to think such considerations don't influence public decision-making?

Am I a conduit for facts or a seeker after truth?

In an attempt to keep the story from escaping beyond my grasp, I find myself falling back on my own cultural references. Because the Descendant of the Last Chumash Speaker is a member of the board of directors of a prestigious museum, I am predisposed to find her more credible than Medicine Woman and her husband. Likewise, her associate, the Director of the Chumash Center, has a history of working with Anglo institutions. On the other hand, I find myself wishing for a fleshing out of The Traditionalist's story, at the very least an acknowledgment of what the mounting documentation appears to attest to: that he and Medicine Woman fear for their livelihood. The Traditionalist entered the monitoring business early, before others caught on that it was lucrative, and no doubt it has been difficult to watch newcomers undermine this effort. But if The Traditionalist's position is as tenuous as it appears, why not strike a compromise with the Director of the Chumash Center?

Standing in the square tower of the Southwest Museum just north of downtown Los Angeles, I watch the director pull out drawer after drawer of human remains, skeletons of Native Americans removed from their homeplaces to this Anglo museum. The director makes an effort to establish the value of the collection, remarking on the museum's trail-blazing work documenting Native American culture, but he is no easier with these misplaced skeletons than I am, his averted gaze suggesting hope that I won't devalue him personally on the basis of what he shows me. Could it be that for The Traditionalist and his wife, given the loss of so many other sites, whatever remains of the Milling Stone village of Sumo is sacred because it is untouched, and therefore rare?

I am sitting in the courtroom today, blinking in the harsh industrial light, because Malibu's city manager, city attorney, and planning director have proposed a limit on what the Mortgage Broker can be forced to pay for the study and protection of any artifacts that might be discovered on his property. The city's offer is based on a provision of California law that specifies that the cost of protecting Native American artifacts or remains cannot exceed more than three-quarters of 1 percent of the cost of a project, whether commercial or residential. I wince when I hear the offer: less than $10,000 to both study and protect the site, much less than what the Mortgage Broker had initially been prepared to pay and far less than the $30,000 AIM estimates is needed for a study alone.

When court recesses, the thin woman in black who leads the local AIM chapter notices me sitting on a bench opposite the courtroom. In AIM's view, the newspaper I work for has not been kind to The Traditionalist and his clan, and this makes me fair game. I watch Black-Suited Woman gather a contingent of chanting, sign-waving Chumash around her and prepare to lead them in my direction. "There's that bitch from *The Malibu Times,*" Black-Suited woman shouts, pointing at me as the other people in the hallway move aside to give the Chumash room and charging my bench to stand over me rigid, her face a leer. But the Chumash she leads stop before they reach me. Like me, they are unsure what to do.

Sitting in court today, I realize I have long since abandoned hope for a morally correct or ethical conclusion to these events, or for the compromise that might anoint the dreams of the players. Nor are the stakes purely personal. The Mortgage Broker's case offers an opportunity for our community to model partnerships among landowners, anthropology professionals, and town governments that might resolve the inevitable conflicts which occur when passions clash with the harsh reality of municipal law. That this is not likely to happen was predicted almost twelve months earlier at a meeting of the task force that developed Malibu's cultural resources ordinance.

The meeting was set for the lobby of city hall, where there was enough room for the task force to do its business and still accommodate spectators. This would be the first time the group would conduct its business in public, and the Native Americans were clearly uncomfortable with the turn of events, as were the Anglos who served with them and had made it a habit to defer to their interests. The Mortgage Broker's repeated appeals for redress had raised the antennae of Malibu's property rights watchdogs, who were in the audience along with their standard bearer, John Harlow. A rumored encounter between The Traditionalist and the Director of the Chumash Center had increased the theatrical potential of the evening. The City Archeologist selected a chair across the table from Medicine Woman. The son of the retired actor, himself an actor, who as an advocate for Native American rights as well as the task force chair would lead the meeting, positioned himself in the center of the table close to the City Archeologist. The Descendant of the Last Chumash Speaker, who was not a task force member, chose a seat in the audience next to the Director of the Chumash Center, also an outsider. The anthropology teacher who had taken it upon herself to keep me informed on successive drafts of the proposed new ordinance as the city council subcommittee worked through its revision found a place two rows back.

Dressed in a faded green workshirt and banged-up cowboy boots, the actor opened the meeting, telling the audience the task force's single objective was the best cultural resources ordinance possible. The City Archeologist's wife (from whom he was now divorced) offered a disjointed and impassioned review of the task force's actions and attempted to convince onlookers her intentions were sincere. Her rambling monologue was seconded by her former husband, who nonetheless took the time to repeat it all himself. Medicine Woman, who had come to the meeting dressed in Anglo clothes but with her waist-length hair caught in a shell at the back, tried to keep the meeting from turning into a free-for-all in front of all these people. When it came time for her to speak, she was brief. "All the task force wants is justice for the deceased Natives," she told the audience. Her son was less cordial. Brooding in a black t-shirt and baseball cap, Malibu's Chumash Manager reminded those present that Native artifacts belong to Natives and not in Anglo museums. The Traditionalist arrived just as his stepson finished speaking. He was dressed in a denim jacket and wore an ivory bone in his nose.

Dismissing the task force's rhetoric, the Descendant of the Last Chumash Speaker rose from the audience. "I am here tonight to tell you what I think," she began, drawing herself up. "And if necessary, I will be here until my death and afterward." The small woman's voice echoed under the low ceiling. *"When is this nepotism going to stop?"* Seizing the momentum, the anthropology teacher sprang from her seat behind the Director of the Chumash Cultural Center waving a fistful of papers. "The City Archeologist and the Chumash Manager should not be allowed to do work for hire in a town where they're employed on the staff," she shouted, then sat down as quickly as she had jumped from her seat. But the main fireworks exploded when the big guns faced off against each other.

Standing at the end of the task force table but apart from the others, The Traditionalist asked for recognition. Native American artifacts found in the ground should stay in the ground, he told the audience, in support of the Chumash Manager. "They are important for those who will come after us." The room fell silent, as if the audience was considering what had just been said. On the other side of the table, the Director of the Chumash Cultural Center rose. "Legitimacy is the issue," he shouted at The Traditionalist. "Money is destroying the last remnants of the Chumash." Before the director could complete his remarks, the actor's son pushed his chair away from the table. Like a referee at a boxing match, he stretched his left arm back toward The Traditionalist, as if to push him off, although the man he was making a show of protecting was five feet away behind a counter. The victim safeguarded, the actor turned toward the villain. His right arm outstretched, he pointed at the Director of the Chumash Center.

"You are in my house now," he shouted. "In the white man's house. You must obey the white man's law." The audience sat silent, unsure whether to laugh or applaud.

Superior court judge Diane Wayne finally ruled that Malibu's compromise was adequate and the Mortgage Broker could not be forced to pay any more than what the city manager and the city attorney had proposed, regardless of what the real cost might be to protect and study Native American artifacts on his property. Its momentum deflated, AIM declined to pursue the case further. The city manager removed the City Archeologist from the project, and the Mortgage Broker hired the Director of the Chumash Center to monitor construction of his guesthouse, where he planned to live with his family while he recovered from two years of emotional and financial distress. Membership on Malibu's cultural resources task force also underwent a change; Medicine Woman resigned as the group's secretary, and the Director of the Chumash Center replaced the actor as the task force chair. The city council finally approved a revision of Malibu's Native American cultural resources ordinance, authorizing the planning department to assemble a directory of qualified archeologists and make a list of monitors available to Malibu residents. Despite these gains, the Director of the Chumash Center complained that the City Archeologist continued to steer residents away from members of his clan who wanted to work as monitors in Malibu. So convinced was the director of this prejudice that he resigned from the task force and abandoned plans to develop a museum to house Native American artifacts.

As the smoke cleared, The Traditionalist attempted to revive his business. Emphasizing that artifacts discovered in the soil should remain where they are found to inspire future generations, he began advising clients, "If we don't dig, you don't pay." After a while, he and Medicine Woman also left town.

The Mortgage Broker completed his guesthouse, but not before fragments of bone were discovered on his property. The city planning department halted construction until the Los Angeles County coroner's office could determine whether the bones were human. The fragments, one not quite three inches long, another three to four inches, were discovered on top of the soil in an area distant from where two archeological test pits had been dug. Describing the find, the Director of the Chumash Center seemed resigned, but the location of the bones and the fact that they appeared to have fresh breaks caused the county corner's office to be concerned about their legitimacy. Despite the coroner's commitment to investigate, the matter drifted toward an inconclusive close, and the city finally allowed the Mortgage Broker to resume construction.

On Easter weekend almost two years after I began covering the story and not long after the court approved Malibu's compromise with the Mortgage Broker, a worker installing an irrigation system on his property found remnants of an American flag burned on the guesthouse steps. A note charged that the flag stood for murder and destruction. "We have been raped mentally and physically. Wake-up."

"It was very disappointing to see the flag desecrated that way," the Mortgage Broker told me. Before I could ask, he said he wasn't at all sure the incident had anything to do with Native Americans. "It could have been a sole individual with a bad attitude."

▪ ▪ ▪ ▪ ▪

Postscript: The material world of the Chumash is considered the most advanced among California's Native Americans. The Chumash communities were large by Native standards, their villages home to as many as a thousand people. By any standard, the Chumash were explorers. At a time when most California Indians ventured less than ten miles from their birthplace, the coastal Chumash regularly traveled to offshore islands in *tomols,* plank canoes sewn together with plant fiber and sealed with asphaltum, a petroleum tar harvested from deposits that bubbled up offshore. The Chumash were also stone carvers, rare among California Natives, fabricating animal effigies, particularly sea creatures, from the steatite they traded for on Santa Catalina Island. Except perhaps for amateur historians like John Merrick and his beachfront neighbor Ronald Rindge, who of us in Malibu had any sense of this?

I had a glimpse of what we had let slip through our fingers the day I accepted the invitation to the dedication of the Chumash Cultural Center. It was uplifting to see the Natives' enjoyment being together under the thick canopy of oak trees and to participate in their nurturing of one another with food and company. As sage burned in a bowl on a table in front of her, a woman in native dress offered a few words in Chumash then an apology.

"This is all we know of the blessing."

Wasting Time

. . . .

There is danger in this opposition [natural versus human], and it can be
dealt with by realizing that these pure and separate categories are pure
ideas and do not otherwise exist.

Wendell Berry, *Home Economics*

1995

Six o'clock on a cold weekday evening in the middle of December and
I am standing alone outside the Malibu branch of the Los Angeles
County Public Library. The library is a concrete box, the first in a line of
three concrete boxes connected by a flat concrete roof and a raised concrete walkway. The county courthouse is located in the second box,
along with the local office of the water district and the fire department's
code approval office. City hall is in the last building down.

We have arrived at the drop-off time of year, when leftover decisions
and last-minute business collide headlong with the holidays, civilization's
answer to the terror that strikes at this dark time when the earth's rotation steals precious moments from the sun and we feel safer at home,
around a fire. Tonight the darkness has an edge to it; a cold north wind
pushes the moist air offshore, etching images in straight lines and sharp
angles. The clear air intensifies the line between the blackness and our
human efforts to ward off the night. Streetlights dangling on curved metal poles, red and yellow and green traffic lights, the orange rotating ball
at the Union 76 station appear to have edged up a few watts. Although
billed as rebirth, this time of year is often dedicated to frantic attempts to
complete the waning year's business, as if a gate will clang shut between

the end of the old year and the beginning of the new as we watch with satisfied looks on our pale faces, dusting fatigue from our hands.

I am standing alone outside the library on this cold evening in December because some of this year-end dusting and cleaning has been going on inside. The business at hand? How to dispose of the 350,000 gallons of wastewater, the daily total in human excreta, dirty dishwater, and the outflow of hundreds of bathtubs and showers that is said to be inevitable if the area around the concrete boxes is developed. It is a heady challenge that has inspired a dense sea of oratory and released an armada of kingmakers and sycophants whose motives are only partially obscured by the fumes wafting off its surface. Fumes, in fact, is the issue of the day: the potential, some say inescapable, odor that is bound to waft skyward from a proposed 45,000-square-foot sewage treatment plant to foul the air and reduce the value of multimillion-dollar homes nearby. Hypothetical odor that will thwart plans, almost two years and more than a quarter of a million dollars in the making, to develop some of the most valuable real estate in southern California.

There was no local government in Malibu when Los Angeles County built its concrete boxes on this piece of flat land at the base of the Santa Monica Mountains. There were only 6,000 people living here back then, and John Merrick was still hearing cases in the old courthouse on PCH. Which makes you wonder what the county was thinking about. Some people say the county board of supervisors had in mind a community of 150,000 people push-pinned into Malibu's steep hillsides and scattered along narrow canyon bottoms, a property-tax-generating regional residential center abloom around its concrete acropolis, which now stands alone in a hundred acres of weeds and introduced grasses.

It's important to note that the county's monument to civic expansion was plunked down in the middle of a floodplain. Water off the Santa Monica Mountains combines here with irrigation runoff from the houses above the county's boxes, then flows through a network of storm drains into Malibu Creek, from the creek into Malibu Lagoon, and from the lagoon into the ocean. If a winter storm blows in too heavy and too fast, there isn't enough land around the county's concrete to absorb all the rainfall. The creek overflows, the water table rises, and stormwater from the mountains mingles with effluent from the area's septic tanks. See the suspicious liquid pooling in shopping center parking lots, catch a whiff of the familiar sulfur smell, and you can't help but wonder what's coming up.

In planning terms, the people gathered in the library tonight are known as stakeholders in that each theoretically stands to gain or lose from whatever is put forward by the consultants our town has hired to plan the development of this last large chunk of commercial land Malibu has left. They are here tonight sitting on the Civic Center Specific Plan Advisory Committee because the Malibu City Council has awarded this area special status as a discrete planning unit. The stated goal of this effort is a coordinated approach to development that reflects the community's values and acknowledges the area's natural limitations, which include its susceptibility to periodic inundations of water and mud, the propensity of its soil to liquefy during earthquakes, and the fact that it's surrounded on three sides by residential neighborhoods.

Malibu resident Joan Knapp owns ten acres not far from the county's concrete boxes and has plans to build a retirement community, apartments for independent seniors, assisted care for those who can't live alone, and a medical facility. Knapp built the community's first office building, where doctors and other health care professionals could hang their shingles. Now she wants to offer people who have spent their lives in Malibu a chance to retire here. "I'm sixty-two," she tells me. "I don't know how much longer I can keep up this big house. But this is home."

Sharon and Harry Barovsky live ten minutes from Joan Knapp's property. Their homeowners association sent Sharon to the civic center committee to represent beachfront stakeholders who worry they'll be inconvenienced by traffic and congestion from Knapp's project. Theoretically, the representatives of other area homeowners associations are Sharon Barovsky's allies, but in practice they are also her constituents. Aware of Barovsky's past activism on behalf of Malibu (the sewer battles, the fights against the freeway in the mountains and the nuclear power plant planned for Corral Canyon), they nod quietly as she lays out her objections to Joan Knapp's plans, voicing sentiments some seem to find uncomfortable expressing themselves.

Pepperdine University also owns property close to the county's concrete, and like Knapp, is thinking of senior housing. The two landowners are working on a scheme to combine medical facilities and provide the community a hospital. Under ordinary circumstances a town our size would be too small to warrant a medical facility, but given our isolation and the fact that access can be unpredictable, a small hospital would be an asset. The Malibu Bay Company, the community's largest commercial landowner, holds three parcels of land not far from the county's concrete and has plans for an environmentally responsible shopping plaza on forty acres fronting Pacific Coast Highway, a model for other communities. Two descendants of Malibu's first family, Grant Adamson and his sister, Leslie London, own a small piece of land in the civic center, their share of what remains of the old Rindge rancho. The Adamson siblings want to build a self-storage facility on their property, much needed by people who live in Malibu's two mobile home parks and the crowded duplexes along the beach.

It certainly can't have escaped the attention of at least some of the people gathered here tonight that a solution as simple as a municipal sewer system could solve the problem of wastewater disposal in an area that has an abnormally high water table and is located close to a world-class surfing beach, with a creek running through, and one of southern California's last coastal estuaries at the creek's mouth. Effluent from septic tanks has overflowed into parking lots because the soil in this low-lying area can be waterlogged and unable to absorb the output of five restaurants, three beauty shops, two coffee bars, numerous take-out food shops, two banks, assorted clothing boutiques, a movie fourplex, a bakery, and a chocolate factory.

As is often the case in Malibu, there exists around the wastewater issue a disinclination to verify obvious effects. But Joan Knapp has done her homework, taking it upon herself to research a range of new technology that allows wastewater to be reclaimed in sewage treatment facilities designed to recycle it on-site. For Knapp it is only logical that civic-center businesses should join residents on the periphery in an areawide sewage system. Plus she likes the idea of using reclaimed water for irrigation and to create wetlands and other water features that could help keep the area looking natural as it's developed. (*Natural* is one of those words in frequent use around town that are often applied to mean something other than what they are conventionally thought to mean. Although in Malibu natural is typically applied to land that has nothing built on it and where largely native vegetation grows wild, when Knapp uses the term she refers not to undeveloped property but to cultivated landscaping around what's already been built. Such semantic discrepancies reflect the polarities that exist between people who own land in the civic center and want to develop and those who prefer the area remains as it is.)

The consultants hired to plan what gets built around L.A. County's concrete agree that a small package sewage treatment plant is probably the best solution to the area's wastewater problems. Their experts have determined that effluent from septic systems is a fundamental source of groundwater throughout Malibu, and such systems are far from optimal where land is soggy and prone to slide and where environmentally sensitive natural resources are known to exist. There is the peripheral consideration that Malibu is chronically short of water, and if reclaimed water from a self-contained sewage treatment plant ever exceeded demand, the town might profit from making the surplus available to citizens.

Such considerations aside, Sharon Barovsky and the beachfront homeowners she represents are already on record: they will refuse to abandon their septic tanks to connect to a sewer system of any kind. (A technical note here: The septic systems in general use around Malibu typically depend on a concrete receptacle into which all household or commercial waste is diverted regardless of source, from toilet to washing machine. The heavy solids fall to the bottom, where they're digested by bacteria. The fluid that remains, technically called "effluent," is discharged underground into a leach field—soil or sand or crushed rock—which filters the remaining toxins. Septic tank effluent is not to be confused with effluent from a sewage treatment facility, which is released into the environment cleansed of bacteria and may undergo additional processing to increase the number of applications for which it can be utilized.)

There are reasons for the position the homeowners Barovsky represents have taken in favor of their septic systems. For one, the local doctrine of slow growth holds that sewers facilitate development while septic tanks, because they require land to be set aside for leach fields, forestall it. "Damn the sewers" went the rallying cry among residents who rode buses downtown with antidevelopment activists Carolyn Van Horn and Walt and Lucile Keller to protest the county's plans. If we resist the sewers, the logic went, we can keep Malibu the way we like it, an amorphous condition known locally as rural. (*Rural* is another local code word. Applied in the context of slow growth, it may invoke images of agricultural communities where residents earn their living from the land. In Malibu the term is used to suggest open space and minimal commercial development.) For its part, the county argued that the use of septic tanks in an area prone to landslides, with questionable soils, inadequate drainage, and a string of wet beach lots (under saltwater when the tide comes in) poses a threat to the environment Malibu is said to prize, not to mention human health. Still, we stand by our preference to deposit our waste in concrete tanks, filter bacteria-laden residue through sometimes inadequate leach fields, and periodically pump the receptacles, risking spillage from broken hoses, inept workers, and traffic accidents as the pumping trucks head off to dispose of their loads at—what else?—a sewage treatment plant.

Before these meetings, I never gave much thought to how our town disposes of its waste. True, two months after I moved into my rented house on Point Dume, the septic tank belched and spread a sea of foul-smelling sludge across the front lawn—and the day my next-door neighbors planned their annual Super Bowl chili cook-off, their septic tank burped and Andy Gump had to be called to install one of his portable johnnies. There was also my friend Hana's ditty about mellowing the yellow and flushing down the brown, which I took as advice for conserving water. Before I started attending these meetings, I never gave much thought to the thousands of septic tanks in Malibu. Where does all that go?

In the twelve months that have passed since the Civic Center Specific Plan Advisory Committee began its eighteen-month run, it has excluded automobile repair shops from the civic center, restricted night lighting and amplified sound, specified the height of buildings and the style of roofs, defined the size of parking spaces for patrons of any theaters and specialty shops that might be built, limited outdoor dining, and made recommendations about traffic circulation, the number of beds in bed-and-breakfast inns, and the type of first-story entrances allowed for second-story businesses. It has also specified the details of landscaping, including what should be planted to soften parking lots, and laid out the maximum number and size of parking spaces required for any estate homes that might be built here. Trying hard to maintain a distance from the issues the committee debates with such nitpicking enthusiasm, I have lately found myself caught between two poles, one idealistic, the other skeptical. When the consultants suggested the committee members develop a set of planning principles to provide a theoretical framework for their discussions, I was enthusiastic; less so when I saw the results, which sounded more like a set of traffic regulations than concepts designed to be inspirational. But in Malibu traffic is critical, so under *traffic* I read:

CIRCULATION THROUGH THE PLAN AREA should DISCOURAGE THROUGH TRAVELERS SHORT-CUTTING BETWEEN PCH AND MALIBU CANYON;

under *architecture:*

BUILDINGS should be LOW SCALE. LARGE BUILDINGS WITH LONG, UNINTERRUPTED FACADES AND ROOFLINES are not desirable;

under *wastewater:*

THE DESIGN AND SITING OF THE SEWAGE TREATMENT AND DISPOSAL SYSTEM must avoid NOISE, VISUAL AND ODOR IMPACTS.

The cynic in me has searched in vain for the kind of language that might in fact be considered principled, in the sense of acknowledging the current value open land has to Malibu residents and what, with the correct planning, it might come to mean in the future—or how land use appropriate to the civic center's natural setting might be defined.

In the twenty years since Los Angeles County constructed its concrete boxes in the floodplain near Malibu Creek, not much else has been developed here, which gives the area a by-the-side-of-the-road look. Custom houses have replaced the small tree-shaded ranchettes that once lined the far side of Malibu Creek, and many of the old-timers who live on the hill above the county's boxes have split their one-acre lots, selling to people who want less land and more view. Businesses currently located in the civic center sprang up helter-skelter to serve first the entertainment industry celebrities in the Malibu Colony, then neighborhoods of families who moved here to escape the type of urban living the county once planned here. Two shopping centers occupy space around the county's concrete and provide a place where we can bank, buy a CD, or settle in with a cup of coffee. The Hughes Supermarket moved across the highway ten years ago into the new pink mall, but the movie theater is still located here, along with a bakery and the cheap pizza place. The town's one good restaurant used to be on this side of the highway; now there are four pricey eateries between the two small shopping areas on the north of PCH and the new mall across the highway. Closer to the hills and out of sight is what the planners have designated Malibu's "light industrial area," which includes a masonry supply business, the lot where the telephone company once parked its service vehicles, and the land where Grant Adamson and his sister plan their self-storage facility. Closer to the highway, Malibu Lumber, the community's building supply and hardware store, occupies its long-established site not far from the Malibu Bay Company's field where the Kiwanis Club throws its annual Labor Day chili cook-off and where, in October, a vendor sets up to sell pumpkins and stays to sell Christmas trees. The rest of the year we are pleased to see only the unbuilt field rising toward the mountains. We accept the county's concrete as a monument to the boom that never was.

Even with the boxes and what business is already established here, if you drove by from out of town, you might say the area has a sleepy look to it. People like Sharon Barovsky prefer to think of it as natural. But in Malibu, when people talk about keeping land natural they don't mean they're against moving some dirt around to build someone a nice place to live. What they object to is making adjustments on a large scale.

Because southern California lacks resources typically associated with development—water and fuel and mature soils—the boosters have always sold the climate. The result, never much appreciated by immigrants who hopscotched the desert to arrive in a lush and hospitable landscape, is that much of southern California is an improvisation. Had this rearrangement of resources not occurred, what we now know as the Los Angeles basin, a semiarid coastal plain with the desert at its back, would look much different than it does today. By the time Frederick Hastings Rindge arrived from Massachusetts and was settling himself on his Malibu estate at the end of the nineteenth century, fifty-seven irrigation companies had already been established to distribute water to the dry foothills east of Los Angeles, and when tourists and would-be settlers stepped off trains in Pasadena, they were greeted by a dense sea of orange groves. Los Angeles originally drew its water from its namesake river, distributing its often unruly flow through a system of manmade channels called *zanjas*. Demand grew so quickly that by the time the Pullman immigrants began arriving in force, the City of Angels boasted a pressurized water system. Five years into the twentieth century, a series of real and contrived water shortages convinced residents they might run short, a prospect that so terrified those who thought southern California innately well-watered that they voted to finance the state's first aqueduct, which siphoned enough snowmelt from the Owens Valley on the eastern side of the Sierras to serve twenty times the one hundred thousand people who taxed themselves for its construction. Twenty years later, when city officials feared the Owens Valley supply might run dry, L.A. extended its lifeline to the Colorado River. By the time the Depression set in during the 1930s, southern California, with only 6 percent of the state's habitable land and six-tenths of 1 percent of its natural water, was home to 45 percent of its population.

The Civic Center Specific Plan Advisory Committee debates its issues at the front of the library's public function room. Committee members are seated around four folding utility tables that have been arranged to mimic a boardroom conference table. The public, which includes property owners like Joan Knapp, who have not been named to the committee, along with local slow-growth proponents, environmental watchdogs, property-rights advocate John Harlow (the only council member to regularly attend these meetings), and anyone else who finds interest in these proceedings, sits on folding metal chairs lined up audience-style, as if we've bought tickets to a lopsided theater-in-the-round. The table arrangement leaves one-third of the committee members with their backs to the audience, which further enhances the feeling that a drama is being enacted for the benefit of us in the cheap seats. Sometimes I succumb to the theatrical image and become stage manager and costume designer to the players seated before me. After more than a year of these twice-monthly performances I can dress the actors and prompt their lines. Like the lead in an English melodrama, Sharon Barovsky rolls her eyes and demands recognition. Opposite her, Rindge family descendant Grant Adamson (who by virtue of his lineage should be a power broker at these proceedings) plays a mouse waiting to lose its tail. On the rare occasion poor Grant raises his voice to speak, often to offer some historical perspective on land use, Sharon Barovsky stops him—"We can't go all the way back to the *Chumash*."

But the audience is not naïve. We follow the proceedings carefully, alert to the self-interest that predictably rears its head and is just as quickly shoved back into its box, like a spring-loaded jester that has slipped its constraints. Barovsky wants us to see a quick mind, a firm position. "The community is not going to tolerate any more water being dumped into Malibu Creek," she tells the professional planners when they suggest excess reclaimed water from a self-contained sewage treatment plant could be disposed of in the creek where it runs along the civic center's southern boundary. Politely, one of the consultants reminds the committee that a neighboring water district's upstream wastewater treatment facility is permitted to discharge six million gallons a day into the creek beyond what it currently disposes of.

Having accepted the conclusion that planning cannot proceed without a coordinated approach to wastewater, the committee has examined a range of theoretical possibilities that include pumping sewage north to the existing upstream wastewater treatment plant, tying in with Los Angeles County's sewage treatment facility thirty miles south, and allowing new development to use septic systems similar to those already in use. All of this is despite the experts' recommendation—given the civic center's location in a floodplain and in close proximity to creek, lagoon, and ocean—that a self-contained treatment facility is the most environmentally sound and practical solution to civic center development. The problem is the effluent.

Homeowners on the committee profess concern about what will happen if the amount of reclaimed water generated by the treatment facility ever exceeds demand—not likely in the dry season, when the water will be needed for irrigation and to maintain wetlands and fountains and other decorative features, but during winter, water will have to be managed, stored perhaps or otherwise disposed of. The homeowners insist their concerns are altruistic. Too much water in Malibu Creek could cause the sand berm that keeps water in Malibu Lagoon to breach unnaturally, and this could impact the survival of the tidewater goby, a small endangered fish that has been reintroduced to the lagoon. Good enough reason, the homeowners insist, for the creek to be off-limits for effluent disposal. A cynical swing of the pendulum reminds me no similar concern has been expressed about possible threats to aquatic life from existing bacteria-laden septic tank effluent or contaminated storm water from the civic center's antiquated storm drain system that is known to find its way into creek, lagoon, and ocean. Continuing in this skeptical frame of mind, I recall high winter water levels could also flood the creek crossing that residents on the southern bank use as a backdoor into their community, as well as lawns that front directly on the water—plus render dysfunctional the leach fields that serve houses close to the lagoon. The subtext to all this wrangling, the code if you will, is that if reclaimed water from the sewage treatment plant can't be disposed of in a way that is acceptable to the community, the plant can't be built and the civic center will remain undeveloped.

Tonight such considerations are beside the point. Putting aside whether a wastewater treatment plant will materialize to generate effluent, tonight committee members must select a location. They resist. They would rather debate—once again—whether a small, self-contained treatment facility is really the most practical, cost-effective, and environmentally sound solution to the area's wastewater problems or whether the plant should be fully enclosed or buried or screened by trees, or if it might not be better divided into three miniplants, as one of the architects on the committee has suggested. "We could put the plant over the senior housing," says the representative from the Malibu Bay Company. "That's a joke," he adds, before anyone can object.

Malibu Lagoon and Malibu Creek have not always been so sacred. Not long after World War II, an engineer came to town with plans to build a two-million-dollar yacht harbor in the lagoon where Malibu Creek empties into the Pacific Ocean. To build the Malibu Quarter Deck and Yacht Harbor, Ed Turner planned to dredge eleven acres behind the exclusive stretch of beach known as the Malibu Colony, not far from the beachfront estate belonging to Frederick Rindge's daughter, Rhoda, and her husband, Merritt Adamson. William Hubert, who owned the old Rindge pier located nearby, joined the Adamsons and a host of other residents in opposing the project for fear its breakwater would erode beaches adjacent to the Adamson estate. But apparently not everyone in Malibu was against having a yacht club so close to home. On a fall evening late in 1947, some 350 guests, including Warner Baxter, the honorary mayor of the Malibu Colony, celebrated the driving of the marina's first piling. Two weeks later Turner was dead, some said worn down by opposition to his project. Forty years later, local booster Henry Guttman suggested to publisher Reeves Templeman that without a marina somewhere along its coast, "Malibu isn't going anywhere."

The yacht harbor Ed Turner hoped to build belongs to another era, before laws protected endangered species, before it seemed possible we humans could tip the balance against nature in such a large expanse of landscape, and long before influential Malibuites began affecting knowledge of the natural functions of Malibu Creek and Lagoon. Today Malibu Lagoon is one of the few coastal estuaries to survive development, and the creek that feeds it is host to the last reliable run of the southern California steelhead trout.

Federal and state biologists and resource managers have encouraged Malibu to be more proactive about the health of the creek and the lagoon, but the community is not alone in its effect on the well-being of these aquatic resources. Just north of the civic center, the Las Virgenes Municipal Water District's wastewater treatment facility treats sewage from 87,000 residents in the Conejo Valley on the far side of the Santa Monica Mountains. The district sells what reclaimed water it can for irrigation, but what remains goes into Malibu Creek. Increases in discharge amounts that reflect the district's growing customer base have caused concerns about the goby, which is exposed to an increased threat from predators when unnaturally high water breaches the mouth of Malibu Lagoon. Biologists also worry that nutrients in the reclaimed water cause algae to bloom in the creek, which decreases the amount of oxygen available to aquatic life, including the endangered trout.

On another front, since the 1980s there have been regular reports of higher-than-normal eye, ear, skin, and respiratory infections among surfers who frequent the ocean just east of Malibu Lagoon, a development that prompted the Malibu chapter of the Surfrider Foundation to sponsor its 1997 Malibu Creek Watershed Conference. While some environmentalists and Malibu residents took the occasion to once again blame the Las Virgenes Municipal Water District's wastewater treatment facility for whatever ails sufferers, state and federal biologists were quick to point out that Malibu Creek drains 105 square miles of watershed, which is home to some two thousand horses as well as populations of deer, rabbits, bobcats, and coyotes and receives bacteria-laden urban storm water runoff from four upstream communities.

Farther north past the Las Virgenes facility, residents in the community of Monte Nido have found themselves embroiled in a campaign against a community of Tokyo Buddhists with plans to expand a small campus in the Santa Monica Mountains into 3,500-student Soka University. The project includes a half-million square feet of buildings. This will require moving 100,000 cubic yards of earth, and opponents fear the grading will produce sediment to clog Malibu Creek. Still farther upstream, residents in neighboring Calabasas are fighting Ahmanson Ranch, a three-thousand-home, two-golf-course mini-city that will require six years of grading (over forty football fields of dirt), posing an additional threat of sedimentation in both the creek and Malibu Lagoon. Runoff from project roads and other paved surfaces, mixed with pesticides from the golf courses, has further potential to degrade both aquatic resources that bear Malibu's name. Although civic center committee members may be well-intentioned when they insist no additional effluent be deposited in Malibu Creek, this view sidesteps opportunities to address a myriad of actual regional factors that affect the stream's well-being while making much to do about a hypothetical local threat.

"Why can't we leave it the way it is?" The question came from a young woman in jeans and sandals leaning against the cinder block wall in the John L. Webster Middle School auditorium. All the seats in the center of the room were occupied, but even if there had been an empty place, it was obvious this young woman would not have accepted it. Given the chance, most people sit at public meetings, although occasionally someone's back hurts or, like me, a person will stand to take the temperature of the audience. Some people stand because they have arrived with a purpose; the young woman in blue jeans and sandals was one of these. She stared directly at the front of the room, where two watercolor renderings of the consultants' proposal for the civic center hung next to a black-and-white drawing. One of the watercolors depicted the civic center fully fleshed out with buildings and sidewalks and gardens. The second showed only roads, what the consultants refer to as the circulation pattern. The single black-and-white drawing depicted the area the way the young woman prefers it: empty, with only the natural landforms displayed.

The consultant who chairs the Civic Center Specific Plan Advisory Committee meetings is here at Webster School this evening prepared to lead the discussion—bright, earnest, and doing his best to sell his conviction that Malibu's civic center can be developed in a way that residents can "buy into." He wants us to believe the planning concepts that have guided his design team have been implemented with great sensitivity to the community's interests. As might be predicted, the people who arrived early and found seats at the child-size folding tables in the center of the room are the first to ask questions. One woman wants to know about ball fields—where will the kids play baseball and soccer? Someone else offers an opinion about architecture: Mission style is okay, but what about something a little more... ah... more... Other people raise concerns about traffic and noise; some worry the proposed movie theaters will draw undesirable elements from outside the community, others that the consultants have planned too many visitor-serving uses (*visitor-serving* being code for "tourist").

The young woman in the blue jeans leaning against the wall in the auditorium of Webster Middle School gives the impression she hasn't heard much of what the consultant has had to say. She clutches a loose-leaf notebook to her chest, pulling the lined pages close, then drops the notebook to her side, then finally lays it open on the floor in front of her. When the question-and-answer period begins, she raises her hand and is patient while the consultant works the other side of the room. When he finally turns in her direction, she points to the black-and-white drawing. "Why can't we leave it without anything on it?" The consultant's voice betrays his impatience. The civic center is private property. "The community would have to buy it and it would be very, very expensive."

The consultant's opinion aside, I know that at least one person in the room has considered the possibility the land in the civic center might be purchased and preserved as the community's antidevelopment activists desire. Sharon Barovsky's husband, Harry, who has served Malibu for the past two years on the planning commission, confided as much to me twelve months earlier when I asked why we hadn't followed the lead of communities like Southampton on Long Island, where residents have twice voted for multimillion-dollar bond measures to purchase out-of-production potato fields and protect them from subdivisions, or celebrities and second-home owners on Martha's Vineyard in Massachusetts, who assembled a war chest to purchase farmland when their neighbors want to sell. Harry had agreed that buying the land in the civic center was a reasonable idea, but planning had to come first. But what was the point of spending hundreds of thousands of dollars planning a project that would never be built? Perhaps the thought was that once residents saw what could be built, they would be more inclined to fork over the cash to keep this from happening. Or perhaps this planning process was a ruse, the goal to soften property owners to sell for less.

The cash value of the land in Malibu's civic center has little meaning for the young woman in blue jeans. She has no empathy for any dreams Joan Knapp might entertain, and little understanding of how her own preservationist scenario might play out. Does she believe, for example, that Knapp, who has owned her civic center property for over twenty years, should just give up and walk away?

I thought of the night Knapp presented a model of her plans to the city council. She had happily circled the three-dimensional model, carefully explaining the rationale for the project, pointing with stubby fingers to where buildings would be situated, providing more information than council members were interested in—like a grandmother displaying her knitting. I recall that her voice rose to a higher pitch when she spoke about using reclaimed water and how this would facilitate landscaping, and that toward the end of her presentation she glanced shyly sideways at the model, then at the city council members and the audience. Then she grinned. She wanted to apologize, she told us. Her dog had eaten the tops off the pine trees, up there where the land sloped behind the buildings. As she pointed to the wire trees, I wondered if this might be the area reserved for her hospital.

When this process began almost two years ago, I had hopes that professional planners might be able to do what our civic leaders, now five years into managing our community, hadn't been able to accomplish: balance the priorities. The consultants know how to interpret what a community means when it indicates a preference for one type of land use over another. They know what's legal. They have seen this fear before, this reluctance to step off into the unknown. Harry Barovsky, who has made it a point to attend these committee meetings (where he stands at the back of the room, arms folded across his chest), tells me this effort is precedent-setting. Never before have residents and developers agreed to sit down and talk to each other. But does the planning commission really believe the people who own property they want to develop in the civic center and the homeowners who don't want to see this happen are engaged in a dialogue? And by whose standards does one call Joan Knapp with her ten acres, or Grant Adamson and his sister, developers?

When I asked the consultants whether they were comfortable with such a high level of citizen input, they acknowledged that while most of the committee members are far from expert in the subjects they presume to comment on, their feeling for what they like or dislike has merit. The consultants tell me they need to know what Malibu is about: "We are the repository of your ideas." But whose ideas exactly? So much of what the homeowners advocate has the feel of self-interest. Residents on the hill above the county's concrete boxes don't want bright lights at night or their view spoiled by rooftop air conditioning units and restaurant kitchen vents. Condominium owners on the flats next to the civic center want guarantees no raucous music will float their way on mellow Saturday afternoons. In the plans they have presented for their individual projects, the commercial property owners have demonstrated that they bring to the table an ability to conceptualize, to shape a rationale and compromise on execution. Yet throughout these proceedings they have allowed themselves to be drawn into exasperating discussions of decibels and square feet, a numbing debate in which the figures always get smaller.

Anxious to bring the wastewater discussion to a close, Sharon Barovsky announces she is prepared to make a motion. Barovsky argues for a show of hands, but the representative of homeowners on the south side of Malibu Creek prefers that members rank their preferences on paper and the consultants tally the results. Barovsky's eyes narrow: "I want my constituents to know how I voted." A show of hands is agreed upon, and Barovsky moves that the sewage plant be located on Joan Knapp's property, which is situated beyond the civic center's main traffic pattern, is large enough to accommodate the proposed facility, and is far enough away from other development that prevailing winds will carry odor away from sensitive noses. The committee passes the motion seven to three. The representative of homeowners who live across the creek from Knapp's land predictably votes against it. What will residents in his neighborhood tell guests when they visit—that they live across the creek from a sewage treatment plant?

Dressed today to celebrate the season in a red sweater with three glittering Christmas ornaments floating across her ample chest, Joan Knapp sits near the back of the room in front of a children's mural that has slipped off the wall and pooled in a heap on the floor. I turn to check for a reaction, but the landlord of Malibu's new sewage treatment facility appears nonplused. Perhaps Knapp anticipates that the development bonuses she will receive for agreeing to locate the plant on her property will increase the density she is allowed when it comes time to build her senior-living facility, and this will make the units more appealing. (If this is the case, she's wrong. In a subsequent meeting, the committee will specify a building density for Knapp's property that will make it impossible for her to build as planned.)

Throughout the meeting, I have been staring at the familiar profile of a man I often see at town meetings but have never spoken to. Dressed as always in neatly pressed slacks and matching golf shirt (among a population typically turned out in sandals and Hawaiian shirts), Michael LaBerge offers to share his map of the proposed sites for the sewage treatment plant.

"You weren't here at the beginning of the meeting?" he asks me, and

I nod. "So you didn't hear what Sharon Barovsky had to say?" But committee member Barovsky turns out to be the reason I am standing outside the library on this cold evening in the middle of December. It seems she insisted on reading into the minutes of the last committee meeting a correction to my newspaper's account of an encounter between herself and Joan Knapp.

"I resent being called greedy and avaricious," Knapp had objected from her cheap seat two weeks before to a remark Barovsky had let drop in a discussion on floor area ratios. Rumor had it that Harry called the editor of the paper to demand a retraction and Sharon herself telephoned Joan to apologize. But now here is Mrs. Barovsky standing in front of me glaring. She wants to know if I am the woman from the newspaper. Up close her eyes shift, and I wonder why it hasn't occurred to her that there might be press at these meetings. I give her my name and confirm that yes, I am a journalist working for *The Malibu Times*. Harry paces back and forth on our left, hands clasped behind his back, eyes on his feet.

Satisfied that I am who she thinks I am, Sharon wants to know why I repeated the exchange between herself and Joan Knapp. I tell her the remarks were newsworthy.

But why had I reported the offhand quip and the umbrage it provoked? Of everything that took place at the meeting, why had I chosen to highlight the exchange between the two women? On the surface I took the encounter as an example of the chasm that exists in the civic center planning process and the failure, or disinclination, of both sides to bridge this gap. But the altercation also struck a personal chord. Over the past eighteen months, the idealist who sometimes guides my thoughts has begun to lose ground to the cynic, who has lately found much grist for the mill. Does disagreement with another person's position mandate that we diminish that individual personally or their values? What do homeowners on the committee expect will occur as a result of the effort they are investing in these meetings? If their intentions are sincere and they are prepared to accept development as long as it can be controlled, do they actually believe civic center property owners will be content with the restrictions they're suggesting? And what of the community's environmental resources? This long debate about effluent disposal from a hypothetical sewage treatment facility has obscured the fact that many committee members are holding fast to septic tanks as the best way to dispose of civic center wastewater and seem to have failed to consider the overall health of the creek, lagoon, and ocean.

Mrs. Barovsky insists that I am wrong; she did not say what I reported. When this fails to elicit a response, she attempts to convince me the remark was a joint effort of the committee—everyone had a hand in it. Finally exasperated at her failure to draw me in, she offers what apparently seems the most plausible explanation:

"It was a joke."

I suspect sewage will never be treated on Joan Knapp's ten acres. Despite the consultants' determination to develop a plan that is workable and will minimize lawsuits from property owners who feel boxed in, I suspect what will eventually be built around the county's concrete acropolis will be a hodgepodge decided in the courts. I also realize I have done my new friend Michael LaBerge a disservice. Dressed in his carefully chosen attire, attentive to whatever discussion is at hand, he represents another aspect of the debate. Recalling that he owns a small piece of property in west Malibu, far removed from the civic center, I wonder why he attends these meetings. Michael answers my question before I can ask. "People like me are not like the people inside the library," he tells me. "I don't have a lot of money, and this means I have to play by the rules. Which means I have to be wherever the rules are made."

Michael LaBerge's remark put me in mind of Joan Knapp's coda to her confrontation with Sharon Barovsky. At the same meeting where Knapp objected to being maligned as a greedy property owner, she also reminded the committee that she had invested in the land she owns in Malibu's civic center to help finance her retirement, and she worried that development restrictions the committee was sanctioning would devalue that investment. "I don't see anyone in this community being asked to give up their pension or their stocks and bonds," Knapp complained.

Something in her tone caused me to wonder if her objection implied more than pecuniary considerations. "You are taking away," she seemed to be saying, "work that has given meaning to my life. You are taking away those things that give me a sense of accomplishment."

I said goodnight to Michael LaBerge and wished him happy holidays. I turned and walked slowly away from the county's concrete boxes, my mood as cold and dark as the polished onyx sky.

Wisdom in Solstice Canyon

The only way to protect nature is to manage it like a business—
in fact to make it a business and devote your life to it.

Robert Redford

Interlude

The message on my answering machine was short and to the point.
"Doris Hoover needs help pulling weeds in Solstice Canyon." I didn't
know Doris Hoover, and I wasn't sure where Solstice Canyon was, but I
returned the call. The voice on the other end of the line set a time for
us to meet, provided detailed directions, and suggested I bring lunch,
water, a hat, and a shovel. But the shovel proved to be a formality. What
I needed was the sharp blade of a short-handled spade. Knowing this,
Doris brought a spare. Doris in her gray Peruvian hat stuck with a
ragged bluejay feather and plopped lopsided on her head. Doris who
liked to talk as we sat in the shade at lunchtime, feeling the salt dry between our breasts. As I came to know her and realized her age, I worried
that the wool hat was too hot for pulling weeds in Solstice Canyon in
the middle of August.

She stood alone in the sun that first day, dressed in white pants and a
short-sleeved shirt and her woven hat from the Andes, waiting for me
with a shy smile. We shook hands and introduced ourselves, then Doris
led me across the creek and up a narrow trail to the cold frames where
she grew her plants. In one hand she carried her spade, in the other the
metal watering can that she used for a lunchbox. That day an orange and

an apple rolled around in the bottom of the can—another time it might be an orange and a banana, but never anything more than the fruit. I watched Doris pause here and there to apply her spade to the soil. The pause, the continuing soft patter, the spade pushed in and the weed pulled out were accomplished in one continuous motion. I nodded as Doris spoke. I watched where I put my feet and practiced what I knew from Santa Catalina Island about spotting weeds and other interlopers among the native plants and stored as much as I could of what Doris told me.

Solstice Canyon cuts through the southern slope of the Santa Monica Mountains ten minutes west of downtown Malibu, one of twenty-two breaks at this western end of the mountains that begin at two thousand feet and drop abruptly to the coast. The natural vegetation is chaparral mixed with oak woodland—sycamores and oaks and mountain lilac, along with walnut and white and black sage, watered by one of the mountains' few year-round streams. By August the stream trickles to a thin flow, but enough to have made it possible for this canyon to be first the site of a homesteaded ranch, then the Roberts family's elaborate estate. When the Santa Monica Mountains Conservancy received the canyon from the Robertses and made plans to open the land to public use, it agreed to attempt an unconventional approach to clearing almost a century's worth of weeds and invasive plants. Rather than trimming or spraying with herbicides, the undesirable vegetation would be plucked out by its roots. The idea was hatched by Doris and a friend in the local chapter of the Native Plant Society. While volunteers moved through the canyon pulling weeds, Doris filled cold frames with seeds for the wildflower meadow she planned opposite the visitors' center. The effort bore fruit. Hadn't I knelt among her poppies and penstemon, smelling the acid scent of deer scat, a healthy sign?

Three years after the initial weed-pulling, Doris and I were now the mop-up crew. We were after mustard, both the pale-stemmed annual and its thick, black-stemmed cousin that persists year after year, and introduced thistles and castor beans (once planted as a cash crop) plus the occasional nasturtium that snaked along in the shade. Once Doris demonstrated the technique, pulling weeds wasn't difficult to master.

You positioned your spade close to the plant or weed you wanted to re-move. You placed your boot on top of the blade and pushed on it until it sank into the soil. Then you grabbed the top of the plant with your free hand and angled the spade against the plant's stem, pulling back as you pushed the blade deeper into the soil. If you accomplished every-thing correctly, the action produced a popping, which was the an-nouncement that you had what you were after.

If you misjudged, if the root was longer than you expected or the soil was particularly dry, the stem of the plant might break off. When this hap-pened, the entire process broke down. You removed your pack, adjusted your gloves and perhaps your hat, and got down to the messy job of pry-ing out the root with the point of the spade, picking at small chunks until you were hot and sweaty and irritated with the whole business.

But when your technique held and the ground wasn't dry, pulling weeds turned out to be satisfying work. There you'd be, spade in one hand, a fistful of mustard in the other, carrying your trophies until they became too heavy to handle and you dumped what you had pulled in a pile at the side of the road for the park crew to collect. I learned early that long pants and boots with rawhide laces were essential—foxtails stuck to my socks and tennis shoes so thickly the first day I had to cut the laces to get the shoes off—and a broad-brimmed hat was better than a baseball cap, which left too much of my neck and shoulders exposed. I learned that without gloves, the palms of my hands hatched blisters from pushing on the handle of the spade, and that a walk in the creek in my boots was the best way to cool my feet. Unless we were working in the shade or by the stream, we ended the day hot and dusty and I always meant to take Doris for a beer at the restaurant by the park entrance. But we always stayed too long in the canyon and were tired or late for another appointment.

I took my niece to the canyon once. She didn't understand that some of the plants belonged there and others didn't. Perhaps she also took one look at the size of the area Doris and I were responsible for, appraised what it would take to keep the situation under control, and with the clear eye of youth concluded it wasn't worth the effort (an opinion, it must be admitted, that was shared by many of the adults who knew the story of my summer work). But Doris and I were adamant. We could look at a patch of ground, determine what we wanted to pull and how we were going to go about it, then lean on our spades when we were finished, ignoring the vegetative clutter that mocked us across the road.

Aside from the heat and the occasional tick, poison oak was our only liability. When the dermatologist asked what I'd done to produce two hundred dollars' worth of bubbles on my right shoulder, I told him I'd been pulling weeds in Solstice Canyon. "Stay out of there," he warned. "Let them cut the weeds."

It turned out there was also some of that. Late in summer, the conservancy imported a crew of teenagers in long-sleeved khaki shirts and goggles, wielding weed-whackers to clear brush close to the road. "Just spreading seeds," Doris tisk-tisked above the whine of their machines. "Just have to do it all over again next year." For Doris and me, cutting weeds or spraying herbicides was the work of a disposable culture. Removing the offensive plants at their roots eliminated the pests once and for all. Working as we did with spades as our only equipment, we were less of an intrusion and had more of a chance to enjoy the canyon. On a Thursday afternoon toward the end of summer, when Doris and I were working our way through a thick stand of horehound, a mule deer doe and her fawn came to browse the grass a few yards from where we worked. We watched the doe and her fawn come earlier every week as the days gradually shortened. In the same area at the beginning of the summer I had found a bird's nest in a stand of white sage—small and thick and tightly woven. Doris suggested that I leave the nest at the visitor's center, but I have always wished I hadn't. I would have something now to remind me of our simple, elemental work that summer.

Nine o'clock on a Thursday morning and damp streaks of sweat are already collecting dirt and sliding down the back of my neck and arms. Salt burns the corners of my mouth, and the lining of my straw hat is saturated with sweat that seems to have all the oil burned out of it. I reach in my pack for my bottle of water and see that the ice I added just two hours before has melted. I drink as much water as I think I can hold, cap the bottle, then drop the pack next to the trunk of a fallen sycamore. The bleached-out scent of mustard and late-season sycamore leaves hangs thinly on the dry air as I check my watch, pick up my shovel, lean forward, and peer into the heat. I am working through the worst of the day, but I decide to target a patch of dry ground next to the road where the mustard is highest. "Dry earth hangs on hard," I think. "Those roots will be tough to pop." Out again in the blazing heat, my movements become less precise. More and more often it takes repeated attempts to push the shovel in at just the right angle. I resist bending low for just the right pull because I fear I won't be able to straighten up to begin again.

For the last two weeks this triangle has beckoned, earmarked as a project. But I haven't planned well. There is the heat, for one thing, and without Doris, I am stuck with a long-handled shovel I've brought from home. The shovel's curved blade isn't sharp enough to cut cleanly through the dry soil, and the long handle disrupts the syncopation I've developed in my hands and wrist and shoulders. I try to adapt my technique by pushing in only the tip of one corner of the shovel's dull blade. Occasionally this gives me enough leverage to pop the root, but most times not, and I am forced to insert the blade over and over. Still the weeds break off. "I want to do this for Doris," I think, "to prove to her I'm up to her standards" (as if I'm skilled labor, an extra body is all). Or perhaps I want to do it for myself, to see how well I've developed this unfamiliar skill, to see if I have what it takes for physical work.

From where I stand I can see the old stone house that Matthew Keller built here in the middle of the canyon, in a small meadow ringed with oaks. Keller once owned all of what is modern Malibu and more, and the old house dates back to the 1860s—so far as anyone can tell, the oldest structure in this part of the mountains. From the outside the house is a beautiful hand-laid fieldstone building, a quiet and solid monument to the past, but inside the conservancy has installed wallboard and carpet for an office, so the interior looks more like a New York loft than a frontier ranch house. Two weeks ago, Doris and I walked over for a look, then turned north toward the Humboldt lilies, the marvelous pink ladies that reign over the thick greenery near the end of the canyon. From the lilies it was a short walk to the ruins of the estate Fred and Flora Roberts built where Solstice Creek trickles out of the mountains, the worst place to be when a Santa Ana wind blows. Up there in that tight space at the head of the canyon the Robertses installed a crude waterworks to direct the creek away from the canyon walls and into a downstream flow to irrigate the tropical plants they collected into this dry canyon bottom. Doris led me past the line of palm trees and bougainvillea that marked the boundary between the Robertses' cultivated garden and the canyon's wild vegetation, then across what was left of a small patch of lawn. Weeds had overgrown a reflecting pool near the steps to what remained of the main house; stagnant rainwater collected in the deep end of a half-buried swimming pool.

There was no breeze in that part of the canyon and the air hung thick and still. Only the buzz of yellowjackets rustled the four o'clock heat. I turned away from the remains of the main house and stepped through the empty metal frame of a floor-to-ceiling slider into the sitting room of the pool house. The glass in the slider was gone and a second panel was boarded up with a heavy slab of plywood. I walked across the threshold left by the empty slider and crossed the dirty flagstone floor. I stood silently in the middle of the narrow room, pivoting in the dirt and broken glass that covered the floor stones until my eye was caught by the brown enamel of an oven built into the wall of the small kitchen area. The door to the oven hung open, exposing the black hole of its interior. I stood there in the center of that small space, listening to the buzzing yellowjackets and staring at the dark interior of the oven as if something might happen, as if something more than this watching and waiting might occur. Off to my left the door to the dishwasher was gone entirely, laying bare the guts and gears of the machine, now rusty and worthless. I stood there in the empty pool house, with the glass in the sliders gone and broken glass and rocks littering the stone floor. I pivoted again in the debris. Why don't they clean it up? Why leave it this way, a gaping hole in this family's privacy? Why not haul it off or board it up completely, this past left vulnerable for the present to violate? But what can a broken oven door tell, frail remnant of a Santa Ana's wrath? What life does it witness? I turned and walked out of the pool house and over to the main house steps. I ran my hand along the layered fieldstone where a section of the living room had been fitted into the canyon wall. I thought of fireflies in blue light, children chasing each other around a swimming pool, adults clinking glasses on a hot summer evening. I thought of marshmallows after a barbecue, the scent of fresh wetness from the creek. I turned and walked back to the pool house, stepped carefully through the empty glass slider, across the littered flagstones, and closed the oven door.

Doris and I are walking down Solstice Creek. Our footsteps plop and hiss in the mud that lines the streambed. The creek's thin flow tinkles in our ears, insects and pieces of vegetation float by. Blisters bloat against the leather lining of my boots, and the blonde hairs on my arm are coated with salt, always and everywhere salt, everywhere dirt and mud. Doris and I are working our way downstream, slipping on boulders. The bottoms of my jeans are soaked and heavy from sliding off the tops of rocks into the water. Doris and I dip our spades into the wet stream bottom and pull out armloads of umbrella plants, listening for the pop as the soil releases the wet roots. I struggle as I carry pounds of plants away from the streambed to drop them far from the bank so the seeds won't spread. Even with a hard shake and a dunk in the water, the roots are loaded with mud. The mud smells of the stream and the dying water plants and the minerals in the soil. The mud is soothing and cool after our work in the sun that morning.

Doris may not be May Rindge, but on this day I feel I could be, tromping downstream, unbothered by cracked fingernails and an aching back at two o'clock in the afternoon when I have three more hours of work ahead of me. Rhoda May Knight was a schoolteacher from Trenton, Michigan, when she married Frederick Hastings Rindge and came west in 1887. She could hardly have imagined she would end her days as the Queen of Malibu, a dubious rank for which land was the qualifier.

While her husband wasted little time establishing himself in the Los Angeles business community (Frederick founded the Conservation Life Insurance Company, invested in real estate, served a stint as vice president of the Union Oil Company and as a director of the Los Angeles Edison Electric Company), May Rindge devoted herself to sons Samuel and Frederick Jr. and daughter Rhoda, and the private oasis the Rindges established behind the Santa Monica Mountains, where they could live quietly with their children amid a menagerie of chickens, ducks, goats, sheep, pigs, horses, dogs, and a donkey named Don Quixote. But the royal edict was running out even then for owners of large tracts of private land in southern California. The first crack in the Rindges' comfortable life came just twelve years after Frederick established his rancho when the Southern Pacific Railroad applied to the Interstate Commerce Commission for permission to establish a line between Santa Monica and Santa Barbara across the Rindge property. Invoking a little-known law that prohibited duplication of an existing rail line, Frederick sought to counter the threat by building his own railroad. When her husband died before the plan could be brought to fruition, May assumed the task of finalizing the route and laying track. Three years after her husband's death, as flappers danced the Charleston back east, May Rindge christened the Hueneme, Malibu and Port Los Angeles Railway, fifteen miles of standard gauge track that ran from the far western end of Rancho Malibu past the private Rindge pier near the ranch center to its eastern boundary at Las Flores Canyon. A White gasoline engine pushed flatcars of hides and grain along the beach and across wooden trestles, some a hundred feet above the sand. The initial fifteen miles of track was to be the foundation for a line to link Port Hueneme in Ventura County, a receiving port for goods off the ranches on the Channel Islands, with the port at Santa Monica. But even as May completed her railroad and laid plans to extend its reach, her ranch was threatened from another quarter when the federal government, acting on behalf of nearby homesteaders who wanted access across the Rindge property, demanded that she remove fences her husband had installed to protect the family's privacy. May's reaction was typically royal: she sued the government. A federal judge ruled in May's favor, but the reprieve turned out to be short-lived. The state of California was next, staking claim to the private road that ran along the Rindge beachfront. Again May resisted. Again the court ruled in her favor, and again the time for savoring victory was short. Los Angeles County would succeed where the state had failed, securing a court order that condemned a right of way across the Rindge property. If May wouldn't allow the public onto her land in Pullman coaches, the county would pave the way for their automobiles. Defeated in court this time, May Rindge responded in the only way that seemed to remain to her. When county crews showed up to survey the new highway, ranch guards locked out their automobiles, forcing the surveyors to carry their equipment on foot.

It was in consideration of such actions that the black-frocked woman who rode the coast road to Santa Monica in a fringed surrey behind a team of matching white horses was portrayed in the local press as an autocrat indifferent to the needs of the larger community. May responded with advertisements in the same papers offering an upland alternative to the beach road the county coveted. But the die was cast. On November 3, 1921, enthusiastic residents of Santa Monica and Ocean Park fired up their tin lizzies and invaded Rancho Malibu through the old gate at Las Flores Canyon. Construction on a state highway began two years later along a route that all but duplicated the county road. Once again misreading her options, May sued the state—and for a second time the court ruled against her, leaving the besieged queen to the old shoot-'em-up routine. This time forty armed cowboys held out against state road crews for three days, an effort that was more show than substance. In 1929 Roosevelt Highway (later Pacific Coast Highway) was completed, and the Oxnard–Santa Monica Road, as the segment across May's ranch was known locally, was heralded as the final link in the coastal route that joined Mexico with Canada. The ribbon-cutting ceremony was graced by Miss Phylys Petit of Oxnard, who appeared on behalf of Canada, and a Miss Watt from Santa Monica, dressed to represent Mexico in a three-tiered ruffled skirt and Spanish-style headdress. During the first sixteen hours of operation, more than 21,000 cars took a spin over the new road, an enthusiastic display of California's affection for the automobile that resulted in two deaths and three injuries.

In a quick about-face, May Rindge set out to exploit the highway. In partnership with her daughter, Rhoda, she established the Marblehead Land Company, named after the family's favorite vacation spot in the East (to which the Rindges once traveled in a private railroad car), and offered entertainment industry celebrities the opportunity to lease property and build summer homes on her beach. Ronald Colman and Dolores del Rio built bungalows on May's sand, as did Jackie Coogan, Gloria Swanson, Gary Cooper, and Bing Crosby, who vacationed at One Malibu Colony in the 1930s. Eventually overburdened with legal expenses—the widowed Mrs. Rindge was said to have spent so much time at the law firm of O'Melveny & Myers that she was assigned her own attorney—and with a declining market for her ranch products, May offered her leaseholders the opportunity to buy the property their cottages were built on, then went on to exploit the Hollywood cachet by subdividing a less attractive stretch of beach south of where the celebrities were established. But time was running out for Malibu's beleaguered queen. There had been first a federal court order in 1926 which required that May liquidate the bonded indebtedness of the ranch, with the entire estate eventually falling under the jurisdiction of a board of court-appointed directors, then the Rindge offer to transfer ownership of the rancho to Los Angeles County in payment of back taxes (the county declined), and finally, in 1941, an agreement with Louis Busch Sr. to liquidate what remained of the property, no easy sell given Malibu's "water problem" and the fact that no utilities had been installed on the land Busch was engaged to market. But Louie Busch was enthusiastic, and in six years he sold nine million dollars' worth of Marblehead Land Company property, so that not long after the end of World War II only twenty percent of the Rindges's original seventeen-thousand-acre Rancho Malibu remained.

With her land her most important asset as well and her most pressing liability, and searching for ways in which it might be made to turn a profit, May Rindge established a small pottery factory on the beach at Corral Canyon, where clay from the ranch was transformed into decorative tiles to accent the Mediterranean and Spanish architecture then in vogue in southern California. Gasoline for the plant's three kilns was trucked into Malibu over the new highway, and the facility's hundred-plus employees commuted to work along the same route by which the pottery's finished products were delivered to the company's Los Angeles showroom on Larchmont Avenue. At its peak, Malibu Potteries produced thirty thousand tiles a month, filling commissions for private homes and civic buildings as grand as Los Angeles City Hall. Although there were dozens of companies producing tile and pottery throughout California during the 1920s and '30s, the work of Malibu Potteries and Catalina Clay Products, founded by William Wrigley Jr. on Santa Catalina Island, remain favorites among collectors for their soundness of design and excellence in execution. In Malibu, pottery employees took time out from glazing and firing for a stroll or gallop on the beach, and operating manager Rufus B. Keeler lived for a while in a tent close to the waves. In 1929, when Rhoda Rindge and Merritt Adamson built their beachfront estate on Vaquero Hill just east of the Malibu Lagoon, they included so many tiles in the main house and in the pool area that some historians have suggested the estate may have functioned as a secondary Malibu Potteries showroom. May herself commissioned pieces from the plant, including a Persian rug for the castle she planned above the old Rindge ranch headquarters in Malibu Canyon.

But the effort was doomed. In 1931, just five years after the factory began operations, a fire in the clay preparation room destroyed much of the facility. Determined at first to rebuild, May was thwarted by the depression, and the pottery factory closed for good a year later. What was left of the inventory was stored in her unfinished estate house, where it remained until forty years later when a wildfire destroyed both the building and tile. The Queen of Malibu died in 1941, without funds and with what remained of her land in debt. Daughter Rhoda continued the liquidation of what was left of the ranch holdings until, twenty years after her mother's death, the family retained control over only four thousand of the original Rindge acres.

In 1892 when Frederick Hastings Rindge purchased Rancho Malibu Topanga y Sequit from the family of Matthew Keller, it was one of the last Spanish land grants still intact. Europeans first explored this isolated area in 1776 when the expedition of Juan Bautista de Anza, on its way north, rested near what is now Malibu's civic center, taking fresh water from the creek that is today a centerpiece in the debate about development. José Bartolome Tapia, a child traveling with the expedition, was so impressed by what he saw at the mouth of Malibu Creek that twenty-four years later he applied to the commander of the military garrison at Santa Barbara for the concession to the land. Tapia ran cattle on his Malibu property and passed his holdings on to his son, who in turn bequeathed the land to his daughter. Maria Tapia married Leon Prudhomme, a family retainer, who did the honorable thing and purchased the rancho from his mother-in-law for two hundred pesos cash and another two hundred pesos' worth of groceries and wine. The deal was concluded just in time for the new landowner to make a killing sending cattle north to the gold rush. But, unable to certify title to the rancho under the new federal land commission after California became a state, Prudhomme sold the property to Matthew Keller for ten cents an acre. Keller reactivated Prudhomme's failed claim and was eventually granted title to the land as described in the original Spanish grant.

After their mother's death, the children of Rhoda Rindge and Merritt Huntley Adamson formed the Adamson Companies to manage what was left of their Malibu estate. What they planned is said to have caused concern among many Malibu residents who wondered what had become of the family's tradition of stewardship. There was first the golf course and development of fairway homes slated for Zuma Canyon, grandfather Frederick's beloved "Zumaland," then a reactivated proposal for a marina where Malibu Creek flows into Malibu Lagoon, a resort complex on the site of the historic beachhouse where the Adamson children had grown up, and a recreational vehicle park above Latigo Beach. Most Malibu residents breathed a sigh of relief when the RV park was the only development to materialize. (Public agencies proved no more sensitive to Malibu's legacy: Not long after Rhoda Adamson's death in 1962, the state claimed her beachfront estate with the intention of destroying the house, an irreplaceable example of California Mission architecture with its invaluable Malibu tile, to make room for a beach parking lot.)

Like other descendants of early California landowners, many of whom were visionaries who developed the area's economic potential even as they were drawn to its natural beauty, the Rindge-Adamsons have had a challenge managing their heritage. Born to privilege at a time when wealth meant civic duty as well as lavish and sometimes eccentric lifestyles, their legacy is difficult to evaluate in the harsh light of contemporary values. Patriarch Frederick Hastings Rindge established the First Methodist Episcopal Church in Santa Monica, founded the local YMCA, and as a nondrinker reimbursed the treasury when Santa Monica closed its saloons. (He also built a library, city hall, and a technical school in Cambridge, Massachusetts, where he was born.) But his descendants have not demonstrated as much public-spiritedness, a reserve that was evident as early as the 1940s when *The Malibu Times* noted it as an occasion when Rhoda Rindge Adamson joined Malibu housewives to roll bandages during World War II.

Today the family estate of Phineas T. Banning, who led the move to develop the port of Los Angeles, is a museum that offers a window into life in late-nineteenth-century southern California and anchors a public park. Banning's descendants have served as docents and as members of the museum's board. In a similar manner, descendants of William Wrigley Jr., the chewing gum entrepreneur who developed Santa Catalina Island as an international resort, honored Wrigley's affection for the island landscape by deeding the bulk of the family's holdings to a nonprofit conservancy with the mandate that the land be preserved in its natural state and kept available for public use. While the circumstances that culminated in the establishment of the Santa Catalina Island Conservancy were similar to those that dogged May Rindge's descendants—the levying of a federal income tax, rising Los Angeles County property taxes, and the need to develop recreational opportunities for southern California's expanding population—the Rindge-Adamsons have not appeared as visionary as the Bannings or the Wrigleys, with the result that today Malibu has a love-hate relationship with its first family. At the same time Malibu's antidevelopment activists evoke May Rindge's determination to protect her land from outside interests that appeared to threaten her way of life, they are angry that her descendants are not more sensitive to Malibu's environmental inheritance. The situation deteriorated to the point that slow-growth advocates attempting to discredit John Merrick when he ran for city council linked the judge to the Adamson Companies' development plans on the basis of little more than Merrick's association with friend and former neighbor Frederick Rindge. Together Rindge and Merrick helped establish the Malibu Historical Society and were instrumental in saving the Adamson house from demolition and having it named to the National Register of Historic Places. Both were among the founders of the elementary school attached to Malibu's Catholic parish, and Merrick was pivotal in bringing a municipal court to Malibu.

In the end it may well be that Frederick and May Rindge's most lasting legacy was their determination to keep their rancho intact. Because of Frederick's quick-wittedness and his wife's perseverance, Malibu is today largely a community of single-family homes—and it remains one of the few beachfront communities in southern California without a railroad track running across its sand.

As royalty of the American West, May Rindge and her husband were able to establish themselves in high style in an insulated world where Frederick eased his physical ailments through a spiritual relationship with nature. "Here in these holy hills," Rindge wrote in his memoir, ". . . time flies, but only as the farm birds fly from tree to tree, not as the lark speeds pursued by the hawk."

But as May found it necessary to dam Malibu Creek to provide water for her ranch, and forty years later the Roberts family reworked Solstice Creek to introduce exotic plants that satisfied their collector's need for a tropical garden in an arid landscape, so I satisfy my vision of how things should be by pulling weeds with Doris Hoover, sharing her dream of restoring land that has been abused through human activity. Does it feel that Doris and I are cleaning up someone else's mess? No; we are replacing what's passed with a vision that suits our time and place. As I marched around Solstice Canyon that summer, pulling pounds of weeds to make way for native plants, as I cooled my feet in the stream and rested my aching back and arms at night, I missed the fact that Doris didn't make a project of what we were doing, that she was content to bring her spade and sprinkling can and apple to the canyon once or twice a week and pull however many weeds we could manage. In spite of my prodding, she refused to speculate about the impact a crew of regulars might have on our effort.

Doris understood the wisdom of cycles. She knew some years you gain more than you lose, and some years you lose completely. She feared that if our project became too large and attracted too many people, someone would wrestle her for control. Still I persisted. While Doris rested and ate her apple, I plotted. I envisioned an army of volunteers sweeping through the canyon, a truckload of Smith and Hawken spades delivered to the park gate. While Doris sat in the shade reminiscing about the yucca plants she raised in graduate school, I battled the urge to allow my mind to rest and take things as they were. I calculated how many days a month it would take to bring the present situation under control, what the maintenance workload would be. I wondered what incentives we might offer volunteers, and how to acknowledge their effort. While Doris leaned against a tree and talked about her grandchildren, the bumper cars in my mind bounced from lane to lane. I was too busy planning to hear Doris say she'd already been down that road and had concluded it wasn't worth the effort. I was too busy to hear her insist she was happy to see what we did in the context of the long haul.

I drove into the canyon at nine o'clock on Thursday mornings expecting something. Out of the coastal fog into the heat of the canyon, I drove along the creek, splashing my tires in the water's thin, late-season flow. Out of the car, spade in hand, unable to allow the simple satisfaction of the work to stand, I trampled my expectations with plans: "Doris, what if we . . ."

"Well, I suppose we could," Doris might answer, as if she wasn't sure herself, as if in the back of her mind she might nourish a hope that an expanded operation might be possible.

Regardless of what our vision might be for the future, Doris and I shared the certainty that what we were doing was authentic because it was appropriate to the setting in which we operated. I knew with absolute surety how I would spend those days in the canyon: the syncopated dance with the spade, the soft patter of conversation, the discoveries that awaited me, and afterward the excuse from further labor as I soaked stiff muscles in the bathtub at night.

The story goes that one day in 1973 John Merrick stopped to have a cup of coffee with the Reverend John Sheridan, the pastor of Our Lady of Malibu Church. Merrick found Rev. Sheridan entertaining a guest who was surveying the population in the western end of the Santa Monica Mountains to determine if the numbers warranted a courthouse. Merrick is said to have taken matters into his own hands, filed the necessary papers, and in due course, Malibu Municipal Court was established in one of the county's civic center boxes, with Merrick as judge. Merrick and the other members of the court—Deputy District Attorney Lawrence Mira (who would succeed Merrick as presiding judge), Public Defender Frank Torcili, and attorney Bernard Kamins—had a habit of brown-bagging it under the oaks in Solstice Canyon, which Merrick described as "the most beautiful spot in Malibu." A place where four men accosted daily by the untidiness of human nature might recover a sense of balance.

I finished the triangle of weeds I tackled the day I went alone to the canyon. I pulled mustard for two more hours after lunch, made a half-dozen trips to soak my handkerchief in the stream and douse my head with water, and developed two large blisters on my left hand because the shovel was too heavy and balanced wrong. In the end, I needed reinforcements. The park ranger drove by around two, parked his truck, bowed slightly in my direction, and asked what I was doing. I told him I was Doris Hoover's assistant and I had set my goal to clean up this triangle of weeds, but the work had taken longer than I'd planned on account of the shovel. The ranger looked at the two piles of mustard I had pulled, each now over three feet high, and the two-foot-high pile of thistles and other weeds, and the systematic way I had moved through the field, from west-northwest to east. He eyed the small plot of mustard that still held firm in the corner near the road. "It's getting late."

My shoulders sagged. "I wanted to get this done."

"I'll help."

I kept working as the ranger searched in the back of his truck for a spade. We worked side by side for an hour, our backs bent away from each other, our concentration directed toward the soil. We finished the job just as the afternoon breeze floated up the canyon from the beach. I thanked the ranger, he smiled. We shook hands and I watched him climb into his truck and drive out of the canyon.

After the ranger left, I made one last trip to the stream to wet my head and wash my face. I picked up the clunky shovel and slung it over left shoulder, took one last look at the triangle—now completely cleared of weeds—tipped my straw hat back off my forehead, and started down the path to my car. I wished I could whistle.

On the Fence

. . . .

No person, no family, no country, and no civilization in history
has remained viable for long without engaging in corrective
acts of self-criticism, self-sacrifice and restoration.

David James Duncan, *My Story as Told by Water*

1996

I know how to build a fence. I know how to run a string line, dig a post
hole, and mix cement, how to set the post in the ground. I know the
cold, acid smell of a cast-iron T-post pounder. I know salt running down
my back and blisters on the palms of my hands and muscles in my shoulders aching from banging the heavy metal cylinder up and down, up and
down. But I didn't know how ugly the fence would look: harsh wire enclosure around a field of wild grasses and old oaks. City-bred fence:
quick, practical, metallic, dirty.

In another place, in the sun of a Utah ranch, there is a fence post that
is a tree, a juniper. I see the flat places where someone has sawed the
limbs and top off so only the trunk remains. I pull a strip of shaggy bark
off the tree trunk and more gray layers appear underneath. The bark
tastes like the tree post looks, tough and crusty and old. A sign nailed to
the juniper tells me the land beyond the fence post is private property:
Keep Out. I push the juniper post—no give. Did it grow here?

Just over the mountains from where I live, a pocket of rural life holds
on in a sea of suburban sprawl. There's a fence post here also, standing
alone in a backyard on top of an old stone wall. This post is black where
it has been seared by flames, and splintered and gray in places where

wind and rain have weathered what's left. From this one post I can't tell how the fenceline went. One single post, all that's left of an enclosure that once held something in—and kept some other thing out.

A fence around a piece of land says, "This land is mine and I can do what I want with it."

Mr. Cataldo's land doesn't have a fence. There's no barrier between the road and his property, no neatly piled stones, no regularly spaced eucalyptus trees. Just Mr. Cataldo's property running right up to the road. But the fact that there isn't fence doesn't mean Mr. Cataldo thinks any less of his land. He has owned these same six acres since the 1940s. His wife bought the property from the Marblehead Land Company, May Rindge's company, which means it has belonged to the Cataldo family since before Pacific Coast Highway was rerouted inland from the beach, before houses appeared on Malibu Road, and long, long before the new pink shopping center went in next door.

Mr. Cataldo says he's always meant to do something with this land, but not until it's time. Until it's time, he's happy to have his property serve some civic purpose; in fact, he would prefer that its final destiny be something that benefits the community. Right now, L.A. County stores towed or abandoned automobiles on Mr. Cataldo's property until their owners claim them. Mr. Cataldo thinks maybe someday on this land, a hospital.

Mr. Cataldo is an old man, eighty-four; his lower jaw juts forward and his lips lie close against his teeth and curve inward as if someone has padded his skin with cotton. Tonight Mr. Cataldo is standing in front of the Malibu City Council talking about his land and his wife, Gena. He tells the council members how Gena loved this piece of land and how much he loves his wife even now—though she has been dead a year from cancer—and how he is here tonight to ask the council not to change the zoning on Gena's six acres.

I had never heard of Mr. Cataldo before this evening, but tonight I learn that this gray-haired gentleman with the strong jaw and straight posture has become a *cause célèbre* in a battle between beachfront residents of Malibu Road and those who own commercial property across the street. Listening to Mr. Cataldo speak, watching the stony faces of the city council members, I find myself feeling bad about his wife and agreeing with the logic that the Cataldo property should remain zoned for commercial development rather than for houses, which is what the city council has in mind. The land is just one lot down from the new pink shopping center and directly across the highway from land zoned for a hotel. I find myself warming to the idea of a hospital. Malibu has never had any more than minimal emergency service and ministrations from fire department paramedics.

Later Mr. Cataldo will tell me he and Gena always meant for their land to go to their children, but without commercial zoning it won't be worth much. Mr. Cataldo admits that his brother-in-law has an interest in the property and would rather sell, that his neighbors have tried to convince him to build houses. Assisted by two of the city council's anti-development majority, they tell him he can build six, maybe seven multi-million-dollar homes on this land. Mr. Cataldo says his brother-in-law is keen to make a profit now, but he wants to keep the land for the kids.

Perhaps without a fence Mr. Cataldo's neighbors think he doesn't care about the land he owns. Perhaps Mr. Cataldo thinks because his wife bought the property before any of the people who now live along Malibu Road moved in, and because he's always been a good neighbor, he has precedent and good feeling on his side. Perhaps Mr. Cataldo missed the barrier that separates himself from his neighbors, the difference in values. Perhaps he thought he could step across the street, shake hands, and all would be well.

The city council isn't buying it. There are too many high-rollers who live in the area where Mr. Cataldo's property is located, too many potential campaign contributions, too many complaints that one more parcel of commercial property will mean too much traffic, noise, and congestion. I watch Mr. Cataldo try to bear the inevitable. There is no way around it: his property will be zoned residential, "single-family medium," one house per acre. Given the lay of Mr. Cataldo's land and Malibu's building restrictions, the planning department figures he would be lucky to build three houses on his property.

The council votes three to two to approve the residential zoning. The solidly antidevelopment councilman Walt Keller and councilwoman Carolyn Van Horn vote with their sometime ally, Joan House, against property-rights advocate John Harlow and council moderate Jeff Jennings.

I call Councilwoman House. "How come?"

"He doesn't own *all* the property, you know." By which I assume I am meant to forgive the councilwoman her vote.

At every level of government, there are legal restrictions that control how private property can be developed. A primary objective is to safeguard the health and safety of those who will use or otherwise be affected by what's built, another to protect the public against development that is ill conceived or inappropriate. But the concept of public interest can be vague. How much of the public does it take to put the kibosh on a project—to quash an ugly shopping center, a too-dense apartment complex, a house that's out of character with a neighborhood? For Councilwoman Van Horn, the culprit is land speculation; when land is considered a commodity to be bought and sold for profit, it is far too easy to overvalue individual rights at the expense of the common good. In the view of the woman whose mother was an attorney and father a California Supreme Court judge, an individual's right to profit from owning property must be exercised within socially acceptable limits.

To protect against overzealous community standards, California law holds that owners are entitled to make reasonable use of their property, which means the right to derive economic benefit—Mr. Cataldo and his six acres, Joan Knapp with her ten acres in the civic center, the Japanese Buddhists with their vision of an urban campus in the Santa Monica Mountains. Overly restrictive regulation that prevents owners from reasonable use of their property without compensation is referred to as a "taking," as if the land has been unfairly appropriated. "Agriculture," says Councilwoman Van Horn. "Agriculture is a reasonable use of property." But what if an individual doesn't want to farm any more than Mr. Cataldo wants to build single-family homes?

As the councilwoman explains it, her view takes root in the historic tradition of common land use, when property was owned and safe-guarded as a community resource for food or fuel or as a buffer against intruders. And although a public say in the use of private property does not seem unreasonable, any more than the idea that some land might be held apart in the public interest, it can be difficult to decide what the public wants and then act on this. In Malibu the public good has lately been expressed in terms of environmental protection and institutional-ized in terms that specify the value of property, whether private or public, as a function of the resources it might contain—an EHSA (envi-ronmentally sensitive habitat area), say, or a blueline stream that runs year-round. And while there is obvious precedent in land-use rulings handed down by the California Coastal Commission to protect envi-ronmental resources and in provisions of California law, environmental protection has so far not been invoked as an exclusive rationale for defining the public good. Thus is Van Horn concerned that when property owners are restricted from doing what they want with what they own, they may demand compensation—they may expect to be reimbursed for not destroying something valuable such as wetlands. In the councilwoman's mind this is nothing more than a form of "public welfare."

In southern California, good and even marginal land has always been in short supply, and thus land speculation and its close cousin the booster are facts of life. Between January 1887 and July 1889, specula-tors attempting to cash in on southern California's appeal subdivided close to eighty thousand acres of marginal land—desert, river bottom, mud flats, and dry hillsides. Before this early boom collapsed, real estate transactions totaled more than $200 million. In 1906, when land specu-lators subdivided the sleepy rural community of Hollywood, they or-ganized excursion trains to deliver prospective buyers to the site, greeted the trains with brass bands, and further inspired sales by identifying every other lot with a sold sign. Back then the public good was spelled D-e-v-e-l-o-p-m-e-n-t.

Councilwoman Van Horn considers that the issues that led to Malibu's incorporation continue to prevail in the community, including loss of open land, increasing traffic, and deterioration of the community's quality of life. "If the real estate ads offer mountain and ocean views, trails and room for horses—if we're advertising it," says the councilwoman, "we've got to have it." On the other hand, this three-term public servant believes Malibu is limited by what she calls the landscape's holding capacity (by which she apparently refers to biological carrying capacity), and which she defines as including both manmade infrastructure and the natural environment. "We live tenuously out here," she insists "but that's the way we like it."

There also remains the important question of how many people must hold a value in common for it to be interpreted as a public consensus. When Patt Healy, her straggly salt-and-pepper hair twisted in an unruly braid, her skirt trailing a crooked hem, appears before the city council or the planning commission claiming to represent the Malibu Coalition for Slow Growth, no one questions her. Not once have I observed any member of the council ask how the organization establishes the positions Healy espouses. Never once have I heard anyone request that Healy quantify the organization's membership or explain the interests she represents. Who are the officers, what are the by-laws, what percentage of Malibu's public does this coalition represent? I asked Healy these questions and got a mouthful of mumbo-jumbo. There's no board, no formalized process for establishing the group's position on issues, no vote. In fact there are no members, just "a few of us" who "get together and decide what our response might be." Thus bolstered, Healy trots off to read her comments into the public record, where they inspire further testimony and official decision-making. In Malibu, no politician wants to offend a slow-growth coalition, no matter what its reach.

A former member of the town staff who advised volunteer lawmakers immediately after incorporation remembers his primary challenge as steering the determined neophytes away from land-use policies that would be legally unenforceable. Property owners have rights, Bob Benard, Malibu's first planning director, attempted to explain to post-incorporation activists—rights that are guaranteed by no less than the federal Constitution. Despite such cautions, one of the first actions

Malibu undertook once it established home rule was to implement a moratorium on all construction within the city limits. Councilwoman Van Horn insists the ban was necessary to give Malibu leaders time to sort out projects Los Angeles County had approved before incorporation, a rationale that had the handy effect of keeping the moratorium in place for the full two years it was legally allowable, although not without negative effect. "The staff's energy was devoted to handling the crisis of the moratorium," a member of the planning staff from that time remembers. "We were particularly distracted by evaluating requests for exceptions to the moratorium, and we couldn't put our energy where it should have been focused, in developing the town's General Plan and zoning ordinances." Antidevelopment councilman Walt Keller, who with Councilwoman Van Horn had voted for the moratorium, was uncontrite. Such actions were necessary, Keller insisted, "to send a message to developers"—although just what message Malibu was sending was unclear.

THE CODE

Six months after I joined *The Malibu Times,* when I made the transition from general news reporter to covering Malibu City Hall, I considered myself on firm ground. I had covered the dispute between Ralph and Lenore Neubert, owners of the Dume Room, a long-established hangout on Point Dume, and Moss and Company, the new landlord of the shopping center where the Neuberts' establishment was located, whose agents thought the bar unsavory and not in keeping with a neighborhood retail center. I had covered the dispute about delays in construction of the new high school, and the controversy about the sentencing of a local cable TV producer accused of having sex with a minor. There were the usual euphemisms ("There are certain problems inherent in this kind of business," a Moss representative told me about the Neuberts' bar, which many locals consider a community institution), but even with that I felt secure that my experience was sufficiently mainstream that if I asked a question in the course of covering a story, I could be fairly certain the person I asked it of would answer in a way I could relate to. In a similar manner, when I was first assigned to cover the twice-monthly city council meetings, followed by the planning commission meetings, and when I discovered that much of what I would cover concerned the environment, I tapped into what I knew about environmental protection from Santa Catalina Island. Conservancy managers, sensitive, say, to public reaction to the manner in which sharpshooters were dispatching feral goats and pigs from damaged areas of the island, had insisted I use language that was literal and precise. So in Malibu it took me a while to come to terms with the Code.

I thought at first there were two codes, one favored by antidevelopment advocates who rallied around the troika of Walt Keller, Carolyn Van Horn, and Joan House, and another in use among the backlash property-rights movement whose standard-bearer was John Harlow. Eventually I came to recognize that Harlow's supporters spoke literally, so that a term such as property values meant what it was commonly accepted to mean: the value of real estate in consideration of certain positive or negative criteria. In this way, school board member Mary Kay Kamath could say that she had singlehandedly raised the property values in Malibu by helping to establish a high school in the community. On the other hand, for those who opposed development, the term was an abstraction often applied in odd juxtaposition with slow growth, another code word that lacked specific reference. So it was that when asked to name the issues that were important in Malibu when she was running for reelection to the city council in 1996, Joan House could say that protecting property values was important "in the sense that if you protect property values [by not over-building, etc.], you protect the environment." Likewise if you build parks and keep up a community's infrastructure, you also protect property values. Applied in this manner, the concept of environmental protection lacks status as a declared goal in itself but is put to service as one of a number of factors that influence what Malibu property-rights advocates actually mean when they refer to the value of a piece of real estate.

When I asked John Harlow to rank environmental protection as an issue of concern to residents, his response suggested that—like Mary Kay Kamath and Barbara Cameron, two moderates who ran for city council in 1996 and lost to the slate of Walt Keller, Carolyn Van Horn, and Joan House—he also lacked an understanding of the Code. What exactly did I mean by "environmental protection"?

"You can't have environmental protection unless you're going to fund some agencies and hire people to enforce it," Harlow insisted quite reasonably. Later in the conversation the councilman was precise: The rights of Malibu property owners (again in the literal sense) were fundamental to his political agenda. "It's not vacant land I'm concerned about."

Councilwoman Van Horn lumped the package together: traffic, development, and protecting property values. Kamath, ever practical, made it plain that protecting the environment was necessary not only to protect the community's lifestyle, but as a fundamental civic value: "Environmental protection is just absolutely crucial because of the nature of the area where we live. This is simply very fragile land from so many standpoints."

It took a while, but I finally came to understand that the term *slow growth,* which was in such common use around town, was itself code for the attitude best described as "antidevelopment." In a similar manner, "slow growth" didn't apply to single-family homes but almost exclusively to apartments and condominiums—and particularly to commercial development, a term that was itself in need of definition. What, in fact, was "commercial"? Movie theaters, retail stores, supermarkets, restaurants, a hotel, a magazine's editorial and production offices, the headquarters of a software consulting firm? By the same kind of alchemy, *natural* didn't mean "existing as it would in nature" but was applied to land that was empty, or "vacant," as John Harlow put it. Another aspect of the Code was the facility with which it appropriated environmental terms that had specific, technical meanings and loaded them with emotional connotations. In Malibu the presence of a "blueline stream" sanctified an area so completely as to restrict consideration for development.

The term *development* itself was never defined but was generally applied to anything that might result in inconvenience to the community, notably traffic and an influx of tourists. As specified in the Code, environment referred to the landscape that surrounded the city ("The Environment"), as if a barrier had been established that separated what was natural from where we residents had settled. In this sense, Malibu Creek and Malibu Lagoon tended not to be viewed as belonging to The Environment because they were fixtures of the built community, and therefore no longer "natural" and in need of "environmental protection." In any case, operational concepts such as ecosystems and watershed that would have included Malibu Creek and Malibu Lagoon as part of The Environment were conspicuously absent from the Code, perhaps because the definition of each was too complicated to lend itself to easy appropriation. In like manner, the term, *environmentalist* was not much used around town, except to refer to outsiders ("environmentalists in Calabasas or Pasadena") or in reference to a specific organization ("environmentalists from Heal the Bay"). The word was in fact avoided locally because it was viewed by some as evoking negative connotations. Moderate Barbara Cameron and antidevelopment Carolyn Van Horn both chose not to identify themselves as environmentalists in their 1996 campaigns for city council, Van Horn because she was advised "to stay away from environmental things"—after all, everyone in the community was familiar with those issues—and Cameron because she feared endorsements from environmental organizations might alienate property-rights voters.

It is in this sense that many of the terms in Malibu's code carried little literal meaning but were employed to evoke an image or to represent an attitude or a collection of attitudes. And it was in this sense that the Code took on moral overtones. Aside from making debate difficult because the definition of terms in which arguments might be formulated was nearly impossible, there existed the very real danger that people using words or phrases based in no concrete reference would begin to think in these terms and thus whatever might be forthcoming from a debate would have little operational value.

One thinks of the effort made by Mary Kay Kamath and Barbara Cameron to introduce new concepts to the discussion of development, and how they were unable to accomplish this because they neither thought nor spoke in code. In any case, even if Cameron and Kamath had been able to translate their ideas, theirs was a doomed effort because the Code was not designed be functional, as John Harlow suggested when he noted that Malibu had established no policies or procedures to implement its alleged goal of environmental protection. Because fundamental concepts in the Code had not been defined, and therefore those who used them or professed allegiance to the manner in which they were employed were not required to be precise, Walt Keller could get away with bragging about delivering "a message to developers" without being obliged to explain what the message might be. Furthermore, the Code appropriated terms that involved specific references and applied them symbolically, often as representative of categories. Thus Los Angeles County (and more recently the California Coastal Commission) could be made to stand for what the community considered hostile beyond its borders. The Code also made possible the kind of sweeping generalizations Carolyn Van Horn fancied. There was, for example, her argument against a self-storage facility in west Malibu because it would draw "undesirable elements." Was the councilwoman perhaps thinking of the argument usually associated with movie theaters, or had she simply lumped the ill effects she associated with commercial development into a generic pot? In another aspect of the Code, generalizations were often combined with abstractions to obscure the complexity of an issue, an effective device that forestalled problem solving. I think of the civic center committee's generalization that the community would not tolerate any additional release of reclaimed water disposed of in Malibu Creek, a statement that *appeared* to be backed by the implication of environmental concern, although the exact nature of the environment to be protected and what it was to be protected against, as well as procedures to guarantee that protection, remained undefined.

Finally, the Code was singular for terms that were incorporated through implication, words like *isolated, separatist,* and *insular,* terms that were fundamental to the community's view of itself but, because they were in the main socially unacceptable, weren't used in conversation.

Given the preference among Malibu's antidevelopment advocates to speak in code, and given the Code's underlying assumption of them-versus-us, and that as a staff member of Malibu's moderate weekly newspaper I was one of those whose intentions were suspect and therefore important to speak to in code, when it came to reporting about individuals in public service, I began to feel myself falling prey to stereotypes—until it came to me that I might assess the range and scope of a person's thoughts by what appeared to concern him or her on the surface.

On the occasion I spoke with Joan House about the 1996 city council triumph of Keller, Van Horn, and House, the newly reelected councilwoman revealed that she had been so preoccupied with family obligations that she allowed volunteers to pen campaign letters in her name ("cut and paste from stock letters" is how she explained it). All this had come in answer to a question about the kind of direct mail campaigns the councilwoman felt were effective. Later, House described Malibu's first city council as lacking in balance and suggested that what was needed was a businessperson—or an educator who could offer historical perspective. This observation was presumably by way of explaining why she had decided to run for a council seat. I recall walking away from the interview with the sense that this was a woman who, however complete her knowledge of the past might be, lacked vision for the future.

Councilman Walt Keller wasn't interested in speaking about his election victory, nor was his wife forthcoming when I asked if she might share her experiences from the early days of Malibu's struggles. Lucile Keller referred me to a fellow activist to whom she had forwarded her files, as if she thought the history of a place could be established exclusively in its documents. Only once did I have the opportunity to encounter Councilman Keller on anything but a formal basis. The occasion was a fundraiser in conjunction with the Surfrider Foundation's watershed conference. At the end of the evening, someone suggested I might drop the councilman at city hall, where his wife was attending a meeting. This was an interesting development in itself, to ask a "prodevelopment journalist" to transport an antidevelopment city council member. But there he was, Walt Keller—gray-haired, almost gaunt ("I run 10KS and *win* them"), insistent, and combative, and obstructionist—sitting on the far side of the big front seat of my Dodge Ram, confiding that he had wanted to be a airplane pilot but his eyes hadn't been good enough. It wasn't much, but it suggested a common humanity, perhaps a vulnerability or a cause for the rigidity and the impulse for control.

When Barbara Cameron and I spoke of the failure of her city council campaign, she had complained that her opponent, Carolyn Van Horn, had not used recycled paper for her campaign literature: "I could no more have sent a campaign mailer out on non-recycled material than anything." Then: "The hard thing for me as a humanist to understand is why it would not be the goal of this community to run fair and safe and honest political campaigns as the highest, most honorable thing we could do, in contrast to what's done in the rest of the nation." Cameron's running mate, Mary Kay Kamath, had also spoken about moral responsibility. "Our community is the laughingstock of other communities," said Kamath, "and this is sad because people who run for positions like those on the city council should be looked up to." When I suggested that perhaps opportunism went with the territory, Kamath, a veteran of three school board campaigns, cut me off: "Politicians don't have to be that way. I've never done that sort of thing."

I began to wonder if the problem was not so much one of scale as I had previously thought—the larger and more remote from those it serves a government is, the less engaged it is likely to be with its constituents and therefore more subject to individual whim—and to understand that in contrast to what I had previously believed, small towns have no corner on integrity.

Myth had it that Councilman Jeff Jennings, known around town as a moderate, was driven to public service by combat experience in Vietnam, which the councilman was said to have translated into an impulse to stand by his personal values. This was in turn said to account for the fact that Jennings didn't cater to supporters, that he would prefer losing an election to falling prey to special interests (this was considered by some to be a political weakness). The danger in Malibu, Jennings told me, was the community's tendency "to be more interested in posturing than in actually doing something that is going to improve the situation." Which I took as the councilman's way of signaling that he was aware of the Code.

In communities like Malibu that are governed by a five-member city council, any issue worth its salt eventually ends up at the council table. The city council controls the town's finances, has the last say on planning issues, passes ordinances and laws, and must certify the town's general plan, or charter. The council is also the sounding board for community concerns. Residents and businesses may bring their case directly before the council and may likewise appeal decisions made by citizen commissions or the town's professional staff. The city council is meant to be the community's court of last resort, which means that sooner or later all the movers and shakers make an appearance in the council chambers, some more often than others.

So it was at a city council meeting on a balmy night in August that I met attorney Alan Block. On this occasion Block was decked out in a lime green suit, maroon brogues, and a matching maroon-lime tie. I watched him ascend to the microphone and, in his high, flat voice, make his case before the council. As if the suit wasn't enough, the way Block spoke caught my attention. His voice was scraggly and high at the same time, and he looked the council members in the eye and offered no apologies for what he had to say, but without going on the offensive. When I thought about it, Block had experience; this was his third year of appearances before the city council. Alan Block selling snake oil, trying to make a buck off Malibu's hide.

Block is not Malibu's kind of attorney, a far cry from the environmental lawyers we're used to in navy blazers and khaki slacks who make their points in charged and serious voices, bent on teaching us something. Except that Alan Block comes from the same side of the street— he earned his spurs in the state attorney general's office defending the public's right to have access to its coast and beaches. On this warm evening in August, however, Block seems to be on the other side, appearing on behalf of out-of-town property owners who have plans to build thirty-eight condominiums on six and a half acres of undeveloped land locals call Trancas Field.

I once rode a horse in Trancas Field. In the soft light of an early spring dusk, I rode with a friend down the front of his property toward the beach just as the last slanting rays of sun bounced off the dark ocean. We kept our horses close to the edge of the field because the light was falling fast and we couldn't pick out the ground squirrel burrows and the cracks in the dry adobe that can trip up a horse. As we rode, my friend remembered how on a morning the summer before, he had just missed a rattlesnake in this field, had caught sight of its shape coiled close to his horse's front hoof as they cantered past.

As far back as I can remember, Trancas Field has been the way it was that evening, open and untethered, its high grasses glistening in the light of the setting sun. The two-lane road we walked our horses down separates the open field we skirted from a subdivision of a hundred-plus houses that has always been out of place in this most rural part of town. The developers who built these cookie-cutter houses on mostly quarter-acre lots enticed buyers with a private club on the beach. Although the out-of-place subdivision had already been built when I first drove out this way twenty years ago, the only other development was a three-story white mansion said to belong to an Asian holy man. Today an ever-expanding ring of single-family homes encloses the field to the north and east, so many houses you could call this a neighborhood. Pacific Coast Highway forms the field's southern boundary, which means that on all but one flank, this open piece of land is bounded by development.

Trancas Field is actually more than a single piece of property. Alan Block represents both the thirty-five-acre parcel nicknamed Trancas Town, which is planned for fifty-two condominiums and fifteen single-family homes, and the smaller six-and-a-half-acre parcel slated for thirty-eight condominiums. Los Angeles County okayed both developments before Malibu incorporated, but we fought both, quibbling, bickering, pussyfooting around the legal technicalities for six years.

How could anyone say they want this land developed, this golden field with its dewy grasses shimmering in the sun? This rolling meadow, small remnant of what Frederick Hastings Rindge must have enjoyed a hundred years ago when he rode across his rancho. Condominiums, they're going to build condominiums in this field. Tell me, who would let them to do this? And how could they? Before I began covering the story, I cheered every small victory in the war against the Trancas Field condominiums. I scorned the property owners and hoped for enlightened minds at the Los Angeles County Planning Commission and the California Coastal Commission. I even sympathized with residents on their quarter-acre lots next door. All this from my armchair, before I went to my first city council meeting, before I met Alan Block.

I felt the first stirrings of unrest about public influence on how private property should be developed the night I heard Mr. Cataldo plead for his land before the city council. Uncertainty poked through my rigid land-use philosophy like a worm circulating in a well-polished apple. I hadn't thought about it that way before: someone owns this land, this piece of property that those of us who already live here consider belongs to us by virtue of our long-standing interest, our reverence. Someone owns this land and has plans to develop it. It was more convenient to think the property had materialized somehow out of nowhere; that it existed in a vacuum, waiting for someone with good intentions to claim it and implement its preservation. But preservation for what purpose? So my friend and his friends can ride their horses across the field, so the rest of us can look across its shimmering grasses to the sun-streaked ocean alive with its bolts of silver? Someone owns this land. What purpose do they have for it? Tell us, so we can decide to be for or against them, for or against their interests, these people who bought this land at another time, with the idea they might do something with it, these people who would make a profit from what is theirs but also ours.

I asked the city council's swing vote what you do when the rules change. Once it was okay to buy land in Malibu and develop, now it's not. "You punt," said Councilwoman House. "You do what you can to cut your losses." Fair enough, you might say, for a developer who has other assets, but what about someone like Mr. Cataldo, for whom a half interest in six acres on Malibu Road might be all he has? And is it only a matter of assets? Is there no dream, no hopefulness involved? Is Mr. Cataldo, with his one piece of property, a developer? What will happen if we don't restrict a person from developing what he or she wants?

What will happen if we don't continue to say "No!" over and over and over? Will the ugly condominiums be built, the houses out of balance with the neighborhood, the shopping center that disrupts traffic and is noisy and disturbs our peace? Is there no middle ground, no way to mediate between private property and the public good? And again, the question: how do we define the public good? How do we sort out capricious self-interest from what will actually harm a community? The worms of doubt circulate. The apple begins to shrivel beneath its glossy skin.

So the first step must be to understand that someone owns this land and has plans for it. Next we must acknowledge that some members of the public don't agree with what the owner plans and have demanded a voice in the land's disposition. But where do we go from there? Do we say, "Please don't build those condominiums because they will be ugly? Please don't build those condominiums because they don't go with the neighborhood, because we don't want to look at them, because they will destroy our view? Please don't build those condominiums because more cars will come and there will be noise and traffic?" No, we say, "Don't build those condominiums because they will harm the environment." And when the landowner shows us his plans and how the plans consider the environment in ways we hadn't anticipated, we back up and reframe the argument: "Those condominiums will harm people." Ah, people, that's another story. The septic tanks will raise the level of the groundwater, and neighbors' leach fields will flood. The condominiums will take water that belongs to residents who are already established here, and if a wildfire comes, their homes will burn.

But what of the people who would live in these new condominiums? What of their right to a view of the ocean and easy access to the beach, albeit from a fifteen-hundred-square-foot condominium instead of a four-thousand-square-foot house? What about their rights to breathe clean air and raise children who will thrill to the sight of a dolphin breaking the crest of a wave or a red-tailed hawk gliding high on a warm afternoon? How fulfilling, this thought of sharing our largesse with others. And what of the creativity that might blossom in the juxtaposition of the landowner's plans with what the city prefers? What of the new models for multifamily living, the new milestones in septic design, water recycling, and native plant landscaping that might be forthcoming from an effort to work a compromise between those who own this land and those of us who must live with what they do with it? What of the accolades for the architect, the engineers, the town's planning department? What of the environmental awareness of children raised in these condominiums so well situated between mountain and sea?

There's a fence now around Trancas Field. Signs tell us the land is private property. In two years covering this story, I have come to understand a key to this dilemma lies in the word "vested"—as if someone had sprinkled Holy Water and blessed another's intent. Having a vested right to build means a property owner has invested sufficient resources in a project in terms of time, effort, or money so that it would be an extreme hardship if development weren't allowed to proceed. I mistakenly thought vested meant there were certain criteria the landowner had met that would be universally recognized. I thought of it as a baseline, a place to start. Everyone agrees: you've got a right to build, now let's get on with the business of designing a project that fits. The first problem was that not everyone agreed the Trancas Field landowners were vested, or else they chose to ignore it. The homeowners who live across the road don't want Trancas Field developed because it will affect their view. The people who live on the beach below the field don't want the land developed because they fear effluent from the condominiums' septic tanks will infiltrate their beachfront leach fields. Those who live north of the proposed condominiums don't want the area developed because they think the condos will rob their water.

Would that everyone had come out and made these points in the beginning, and the landowners and Malibu's planning staff could get on with designing the project to minimize the objections—or opponents could set about raising the money to buy the land instead of spending our town's limited resources to subsidize Alan Block's wardrobe.

"The idea is you can't compromise," said Jeff Jennings attempting to educate me on the modus operandi of slow growth. "If you compromise, you lose your goals. But it's not a question of whether you compromise and cut the baby in half. It's a question of knowing when to be smart, when to make a move that makes sense."

Without compromise, there is only the courts.

What happened legally in the matter of Trancas Field is difficult to sort out because it is not about the morality of building two developments, thirty-eight condominiums in one project, fifty-two in the other, in a neighborhood of single-family homes. Nor is it about the ethics of how a community deals with a property owner whose rights may conflict with what it wants for itself. It is about manipulating the fine points of law.

More than twenty years ago, Los Angeles County approved the development proposed for these two parcels of land in Trancas Field. Based on the findings of an environmental impact report, the number of condominiums in the smaller project was reduced from fifty-six to thirty-eight. Subsequently the developer refined the project design and applied for the necessary permits, and the county planning commission eventually approved what is called a "tract map," essentially giving the project the go-ahead. Eight days after the planning commission's approval, Malibu incorporated and imposed its moratorium on development. At the same time, the beachfront homeowners who live below the proposed condominiums appealed the development simultaneously to the Los Angeles County Board of Supervisors and Malibu's new city council. The supervisors backed off, claiming the county no longer had jurisdiction, and Malibu's neophyte politicos insisted the moratorium relieved them of the responsibility of ruling on the project. The landowner went to court, citing law that requires that appeals on subdivisions must be heard within thirty days of a project's approval. The court agreed and ruled the condominiums approved. Acting on the advice of its city attorney, Malibu appealed the decision, but the appeals court upheld the lower court, and the California Supreme Court refused to hear the case.

Then the unexpected happened. The property owner lost the land to the bank, and the land, the plans for the project, and the county's approval reverted to the lender. It was ten years after the county first approved the condominiums that Alan Block, acting on behalf of new owners, made a proposal to the city council suggesting it might be advantageous to view the small condominium development and the Trancas Town condominium/single-family-home project as one. The idea had also occurred to the Malibu planning department, who suggested that a coordinated approach would enable the town to evaluate the joint impacts of the two developments and integrate their design and infrastructure. In all, Block proposed a maximum of seventy single-family homes on the combined acres, and no condominiums. The houses would be clustered in one part of the property, and the rest of the acreage would remain open space. The house lots would be approximately two-thirds of an acre, larger than most of the lots in the cookie-cutter subdivision across the street but smaller than many of the single-family parcels nearby.

For some council members the compromise seemed to have merit, until Patt Healy, acting now on behalf of the homeowners in the quarter-acre subdivision, held out for zoning all of Trancas Field at one house for every five acres. Taken seriously, that would have meant one house on the smaller parcel zoned for condominiums and a total of eight houses on the combined acreage. Perhaps the council majority agreed with Healy's assessment that in the local real estate market, condominiums wouldn't pencil out and the landowner would jump at the opportunity to build single-family homes. Then what? One house on six and a half acres? In any case, the city council turned down Block's compromise, as it had previously turned down an offer from the bank to build six houses on the smaller parcel, one house per acre.

The rejection of the two compromise offers left Malibu with what the county had originally approved: two separate, uncoordinated developments. Since both were green-lighted when Los Angeles County had jurisdiction, they would be built to county standards—much less restrictive than what Malibu had developed. When I asked one of the city planners if he thought Alan Block's clients might still be willing to engage in some creative planning for the condominiums, he looked behind me for the turnip truck I'd fallen off. Having been vested for county standards, why would the property owners risk further discussion under Malibu's more difficult regulations?

All was quiet on the legal front for two years. To those who followed the story, it appeared the problem had resolved itself and Alan Block and the Trancas Field condominiums had simply gone away. Except now we have Block's appearance before the city council on this pleasant evening in August, asking the council members to undertake the unpleasant task of approving the final map for his client's thirty-eight condominiums. Since Los Angeles County Superior Court has long since ruled that Malibu must approve the final map if it is not substantially different from the original map already on file, what Block is asking for is a formality. Not that the city council sees it that way. Faced with inflammatory messages on their answering machines, bombarded with hostile faxes, the two antidevelopment council members, Carolyn Van Horn and Walt Keller, and their sometime swing-vote ally Joan House have decided they must seek a way to avoid recording the map, because recording the map would obligate the town to issue building permits. After more than two hours of posturing and argument (I remind myself all this debate is occurring after the town has lost two legal decisions and rejected two offers to compromise), Keller–Van Horn–House finally discover they have an option in a state law that allows a community not to record a tract map if the resulting subdivision would pose a threat to public health and safety.

What threat to public health and safety?

The three council members consult their faxes: fires and floods.

John Harlow, the council's property-rights advocate, and Jeff Jennings as its moderate, vote together to discharge Malibu's administrative duty and record the map. "Nobody in this town wants to see thirty-eight condos on that site," Jennings summed up the dilemma. "But if we keep fighting, when it comes down to the end, we'll have no leverage to negotiate."

As the council voted, it was not clear from his reaction what Alan Block would recommend to his clients—go back to the drawing board and design around the council's declared concerns about wastewater and fire protection, or go to court to force Malibu to approve the map. Block decides to give it one last try. Once again he will come before the city council with the information council members insist they must have to assuage their concerns. Once again, the council will vote not to record the map, and once again, the matter will undergo a hiatus, not to be brought forward for another seven months, when the city engineer and the city attorney will recommend the council certify the map. But when the issue does come before the council the following March (Block in white shirt and prudent gray suit this time), the antidevelopment council members throw up their hands and demand yet another review of the data to establish whether wastewater from the condominiums might affect residents on the beach.

Councilman Jennings once again attempts to bring clarity to the discussion. "The law doesn't allow us not to approve a map based on a hypothetical system failure," Jennings reminds his colleagues. "I don't think anyone wants to see this project built, but the law requires us to approve a filed map where the conditions have been satisfied."

But Keller–Van Horn–House will not let go, warning that the condominiums can't be torn down once they're built. "You can't put toothpaste back in the tube," Keller chastises his colleagues. The councilman wants the property owner to build ten units and test the septic system for ten years—after all, if it fails, residents who live near the project will have to foot the bill for an areawide sewage system.

Councilman Harlow wants to know what Malibu would revoke if the project's septic system doesn't function as planned.

Approval to use the septic system, says the city manager.

When all is said and done, the city council again votes three to two not to certify the map and calls for yet another review of the data, costs to be underwritten by Alan Block's client. This time Block sues, and almost a year after the council's first vote not to record the map, the thirty-eight condominiums again go before the judge who ruled the county's approval of the project valid. Again the court rules against Malibu, advising the city council that it is legally bound to record the map. This time the judge takes particular notice that in voting against certification, Keller–Van Horn–House relied on erroneous testimony from two consultants who testified on behalf of homeowners represented by Patt Healy. The judge observes that the geologist who spoke on behalf of the homeowners association misapplied a fundamental groundwater formula, and a forestry consultant brought in to verify that the condominiums would expose neighbors to the threat of wildfire used incorrect figures to calculate the project's load on available water resources.

Alan Block had repeatedly suggested that if the issue of map approval were not swiftly and satisfactorily resolved, his client would file an additional suit for damages based on a loss of $25,000 a month for six years of delays. But with the court decision in hand, Block opts to settle. His client will drop all claims for damages if the city council approves the map and Malibu issues building permits for the project. Furthermore, his client will indemnify the city against any claims related to the condominiums' wastewater system.

You could have heard a pin drop in the council chambers the night the city council voted on Alan Block's final offer. Again Councilman Jennings summed up the dilemma facing the community. "We had ways out of this development, and we didn't take it," Jennings reminded his colleagues. "But sometimes the requirement of being a civic leader is that you have to get out in front and explain why this is the best resolution you can get under the circumstances. I hope the political climate of this town changes to allow political leaders to do just that, because if not, we're going to lose this town project by project."

Even as the Trancas Field controversy ground to a resolution, Alan Block took on a new client, the Malibu Bay Company, which owns the lot next to Mr. Cataldo's property and is facing the same downzoning from commercial to residential use. Although "the Bay Company" expected him to file suit against the city for spot zoning, Block also began discussions with the Malibu Road homeowners association to test the waters for a compromise. But the homeowners were no more interested in discussing alternatives with Block's new client than they had been with Mr. Cataldo. In opposing the commercial designation for both parcels, their representative read a statement to the city council. Mr.

Cataldo and the Malibu Bay Company were fully entitled to make use of their land, the statement said, and the homeowners association would not deny them that right. But the land use must be in keeping with the surrounding neighborhood and could not be allowed to set a precedent for other developers.

When the time came for a vote on the motion to downzone the Cataldo property, Councilman Harlow voted with Councilman Jennings against Keller–Van Horn–House. "The Cataldo property was commercial long before anyone lived along Malibu Road, certainly before anybody who lives there now," Jennings reminded the council and those of us holding our breath in the audience. "To zone the land residential would render it unusable. What troubles me the most is that people are unwilling to put up with a slight increase in inconvenience while they are willing to destroy the value of a neighbor's property and eliminate this family's main asset. It is, without a doubt, one of the least attractive elements of this community."

It has been two years since my friends and I built the chain link fence to have a place to run our sheepdogs. Not long after the fence was finished, the property was sold. Today two concrete-and-glass office buildings crowd the oak trees that once provided us shade, and a parking lot covers the field where our sheep grazed. Not long after the sheep field was sold, my next-door neighbor built a white rail fence along the front of his property close to the street. The fence is open at both ends, which makes it no good for keeping something in or some other thing out. Why else but to say, "This land is mine, and I can do what I want with it."

The Days the Rains Came

. . . .

Each of us has his own earthly paradise, a place and time
on earth where, if we had our choice, we would
want to live for the rest of our life.

Lawrence Clark Powell

1998

In the dry land of southern California, floods have killed more people
and caused more property damage than droughts, which we fear more.
We call them twenty-year floods or fifty-year floods or two-hundred-
year floods, as if we're surprised when they occur. But anyone who
takes the time to check will find that along southern California's coast,
fast-moving, high-intensity Pacific storms—and the floods they cause—
are routine.

Less than two years after the Old Topanga wildfire I am again in front
of the television set. This time I watch a steam shovel operator trying to
keep mud-filled Las Flores Creek from carrying Cosentino's Nursery
out to sea. Not only are the nursery buildings in danger of being flooded,
but the water is so high and thick with debris that public works crews
are worried the turbulent flow will damage the culvert that protects
Pacific Coast Highway. Through rain so heavy it appears someone has
stretched gauze across the camera lens, I watch the steam shovel bucket
drop into the murky stream and come up leaking mud and water. Most
of the year Las Flores Creek is dry, but rain has been falling steadily for
two days, drenching us with a third of the precipitation typical in an entire year. By now the world outside Malibu knows we are not only wet

out here, we are cut off. South on PCH past the steam shovel, water off the mountains has come at us so thick and fast it has cut off the highway. Father west, a landslide blocks the second of our three escape routes. And in the center of town, the bridge over Malibu Creek was closed after a sharp-eyed maintenance supervisor noticed cracks in the asphalt surface. We can't get out of town and we can't drive from one end of town to the other.

The steam shovel bucket drops into the swollen stream, comes up dripping water, swings, and empties its load into a battered dump truck. The loaded truck pulls away, trailing muddy water from its tailgate, and another one moves up in line, but does anyone really think this steam shovel and these dump trucks are any match for a creek that carries Volkswagen-sized boulders in its flow? A friend calls from out of town: "Turn on the TV." I rush to the living room, turn on the television to see an anchorman looking anxiously at the camera: "Las Flores Creek is rising," he warns me. "Malibu is cut off." I hang up the phone, grab an umbrella, and bolt out the front door to check the water level in the plastic garbage cans I've arranged to catch rain off the roof. Inside again, I walk upstairs for a dry shirt and discover water leaking through a light fixture in the bathroom. Back downstairs, up again, I place pots and pans where they'll catch water dripping off the light, then rush downstairs to the TV. In the breezeway I walk past the dogs licking mud off their paws. A long straight needle pricks me in my spine, a slow, hard jab. I turn away from the television and call city hall.

At seven the next morning I am at the public works director's side as he throws open the door to the office where he's spent the past two days managing our war against water, pulls on a yellow rainsuit and white hardhat, and heads out to assess damage, two yellow-clad assistants in tow. Awkward in my London Fog trench coat and mail-order garden boots, I try to be nonchalant about dropping my folding umbrella on a chair. Outside city hall we climb into a van, roar up to the disabled bridge, and stop where sheriff's deputies have parked a patrol car to block access. Quickly identifying ourselves to the officers, we start across. Rain falls in thick, slanting sheets, adding more water to the slick film that has already accumulated on the crippled surface. A news reporter, groggy from spending the night in a camper, presses himself on the public works director. Will the bridge collapse?

If the bridge goes, says Malibu's man in yellow, it will take out the high pressure gas line that's attached to its bottom, and probably the thirty-inch line that carries the town's only supply of fresh water.

"You mean there might be a danger of fire?"

The public works director nods gravely and points to his right, where a utility crew is standing by. We step quickly past the reporter and into a rented Ford Explorer with a rotating amber light on its roof and drive south on Pacific Coast Highway into an empty, monochromatic world: slick gray road, heavy gray sky, slate gray ocean receiving its rain. The public works director estimates that in two days damage to public property has climbed past the two-million-dollar mark—cleanup alone is costing Malibu a hefty $20,000 a day—and no one has had time to estimate what residents have lost. The expectation is that the federal government will bail us out from this latest disaster, but the immediate problem is the up-front money to keep crews moving.

We stop the Explorer to check mud and water gushing out of Piedra Gorda Canyon. The 1993 Old Topanga fire burned fiercely through here, and as predicted, there is no vegetation to hold the soil or capture debris. The muddy water has overrun the concrete channel built to reroute the flow from the natural creek under the highway and has crested the culvert that is supposed to keep PCH from flooding. A mile east, we stop again and watch sheets of mud ooze off the wall of Tuna Canyon. The mud is so thick it has knocked garage doors off their hinges. Farther down the road a state highway crew works to stabilize a line of telephone poles leaning toward the ocean at a desperate angle. I am up to my knees in mud and it's still raining.

The public works director waves to a man leaning on a shovel in the front door of his house. The man smiles faintly and returns the salute, then goes back to scraping up mud that has crossed his threshold and covers his front hall. Jeff Palmer, the town's disaster recovery expert, tells me these houses are built too close together—water and mud back up and can't make it the final few feet to the ocean. Four houses down, a hatchback Honda floats on a sea of mud like a toy boat on a park pond.

Across from Tuna Canyon a group of reporters has gathered around a half-dozen tripod-mounted cameras wrapped in plastic and aimed at the canyon wall as if it might erupt. The media people are bored, and the public works director, standing tall and straight with the blue Malibu seal on his chest, is a welcome diversion. The director of Malibu's war on water does a half-dozen interviews in fifteen minutes while behind him a red Maserati coupe, the only car on the highway, slip-slides toward Santa Monica, dodging dump trucks and skip loaders and spraying muddy water off its tires ("HIGHWAY CLOSED, LONE DRIVER MAKES IT TO WORK!"). As the Maserati disappears, a string of news vans and broadcasting trucks comes into view, spinning their wheels toward the center of town, where the governor is scheduled to hold a press conference.

A crowd of anxious residents watches greedily from the city hall side of the bridge as we park the Explorer and follow the public works director back across the cracked asphalt. It's of little comfort to the citizens standing in the rain that this is not the first time a bridge has washed out here. In 1938 the bridge that carried Roosevelt Highway over Malibu Creek was destroyed by a storm that also closed the roads up Decker and Latigo Canyons and sent three houses sliding down Las Flores Creek as residents huddled in the old courthouse on PCH. Nor is it probably of much comfort to these rain-soaked residents to know that just thirty years before, in the winter of 1961–62, another one of those predictable Pacific storms swept through, drenching Malibu with thirty-four inches of rain, or that less than ten years later an entire canyon in neighboring Pacific Palisades washed out to sea. Striding through the crowd like a field commander returning to headquarters, the public works director is pestered with questions. When will the bridge open? How bad is the damage? When will Malibu Canyon Road be cleared? When will the rain stop? A woman grabs me by the arm: "How did you do that?" When I look blank, she points to where I've just come from on the far side of the bridge.

"I'm with him," I answer, cocking my thumb in the direction of the public works director.

On the city hall side of the bridge, Red Cross volunteers dispense coffee to residents looking for news and out-of-town dignitaries waiting to rub elbows with the governor. Rumors circulate. The governor will arrive by helicopter. No, the cloud cover is too low; he'll come by car. Back in his office, the public works director grapples with the problem of where to dispose of the mud that crews are scraping off the highway. A resident who serves on the California Coastal Commission volunteers to expedite an emergency permit to allow Malibu to dump the mud in the ocean, an action the commission would never condone under ordinary circumstances.

A helicopter lands on the concrete pad at the rear of city hall. Half the city staff rushes out, but it's not the governor, only someone from the sheriff's department ferrying two members of the Los Angeles County Board of Supervisors who join the other dignitaries in the city attorney's office. Each time I check, someone else is sitting at the city attorney's desk taking a turn at her telephone. Since no one in this room has been briefed, I wonder what's being said and who's on the other end of the line. Except for the rotation at the phone, no one speaks, and no one dares leave. Whatever happens, this office will be the first to know. The mayor and whoever it is from the sheriff's office sit next to each other on the city attorney's blue sofa like wallflowers at a sophomore dance, eyes blank.

The crowd at the bridge pushes forward toward a line of cars that has entered Malibu from the west. A woman dressed in a business suit, shiny black high heels, and red lipstick steps out of the first car, pulls a clipboard from a heavy briefcase slung over her right shoulder, and begins to brief dignitaries anxious for a first shot at the governor. "First, the governor will walk across the bridge," the red lips read from a printed schedule attached to the clipboard, "then the governor will speak to the press . . ." Before she can finish, the public works director shoulders his way through the crowd and begins a monologue about what we're coping with and what we need. I watch the woman in high heels scrawl loopy notes across her briefing schedule, hard pressed to keep up. A California Highway Patrol car is parked behind the last advance-team vehicle, then a blue van, then another patrol car. While everyone's attention is on the CHP vehicles, the governor, dressed in a navy blue windbreaker and gray dress slacks and without a hat, slips quietly from the van. An engineer from the state highway department moves quickly to the governor's side and shakes his hand. My raincoat is wrinkled, my wet hair plastered against my forehead, but I am at the Caltrans official's elbow when he tells Governor Pete Wilson that consultants have examined the understructure of the bridge and pronounced it sound enough to open a single lane of traffic.

Moving out in front of his entourage, Wilson strides across the bridge and steps briskly to the bank of microphones the press has set up on the far side. A sea of wet power cables glistens against the slick pavement.

"People are more important than fish," Wilson shouts above the sound of the whirling generators and immediately wins points with the people gathered in front of the disabled structure. Rumor has it that precautions to safeguard the tidewater goby, the endangered species that breeds in Malibu Lagoon—the same goby that sidetracked discussions of sewage effluent among the civic center advisory committee—have complicated planning for a new bridge to replace this one that's failing. "Caltrans will open one lane of a temporary bridge," Wilson shouts to the crowd to more applause. "A new permanent bridge will go forward under the governor's emergency powers. Forget the goby." Someone shouts that the fish are probably off Catalina by now anyway, washed out to sea by the flooded creek. The governor takes a few questions from reporters, backs away from the microphones, and reverses course across the bridge. Total elapsed time: fifteen minutes. "WILSON TOURS STORM-RAVAGED MALIBU. VOWS SUPPORT."

Bloated from his moment in the spotlight, the man from Caltrans signals to pedestrians on either side of the bridge, and sheriff's deputies gear up to provide escort. The dignitaries who assembled for the governor's visit follow him out of town. We are left to our own devices.

Emergency support. Emphasis on *emergency*. A disaster like a fire or flood means money, not just headline rhetoric. A great deal of money. Special funds from the Governor's Office of Emergency Services and disaster relief from FEMA, which means tax dollars from my sister in New Hampshire and my mother on Cape Cod. Knowing what my sister thinks of southern California, I don't ask how she feels about a share of her federal dollars going to dredge Las Flores Creek. Nor do I ask a friend who lives near Beverly Hills and has never come face to face with two feet of mud blocking her commute to work whether she resents her tax money digging out Malibu every few years.

Except for however much of our taxes made their way into state and federal emergency funds, Malibu residents didn't pay for the temporary repair of the disabled Malibu Creek bridge or the span that replaced it. Certainly we didn't fork up the funds from our limited treasury. The fact is Pacific Coast Highway and the bridge on which it crosses the creek belong to the state. The road Malibu thinks of as its main street actually runs the length of the California coast. Caltrans engineers say the two most costly segments of the highway to maintain are its twenty-seven-mile route through Malibu and its cliffhanging run-through Big Sur—and for the same reason: the topography. But neither in our town nor in Big Sur have residents ever been assessed an extra dollar to support these disproportionately expensive sections of highway.

By the same token, Pacific Coast Highway is more than Malibu's main route in and out. The 55,000 vehicle trips a day that pass through include tourists from Omaha (ask them if they're happy their tax dollars helped rebuild the Malibu Creek bridge) and commuters heading south and west into Los Angeles. During the morning rush almost three-quarters of the cars on PCH are carrying commuters, some from as far away as Camarillo, thirty miles north of us, who leave the Ventura Freeway and cross the Santa Monica Mountains on Kanan Dume Road or Malibu Canyon Road to take Pacific Coast Highway into the city.

Los Angeles County built Kanan Dume Road not long after it constructed its concrete boxes in the floodplain next to Malibu Creek. Malibu Canyon Road had already been built, following a break in the mountains known to the Chumash and no doubt to homesteaders who crossed the Rindge ranch on their way to Santa Monica. Even as it was being planned, Kanan Dume Road drew criticism. Some residents worried that the new highway would open the undeveloped beaches of Malibu's west end to an influx of summer visitors from the San Fernando Valley (hence the "Vals Go Home" signs spray-painted on rocks along its route). Others expressed concern that the highway would be difficult to maintain. The name locals apply to Los Angeles County Route N9 reflects its fifteen-mile run from Point Dume in Malibu to Agoura Hills on the other side of the mountains, where the Kanan family once settled. Some people in Malibu call it Dume Kanan Road, putting the priorities where they belong.

Practically speaking, Kanan Dume Road is a conventional asphalt surface laid over a gravel roadbed constructed through a patchwork of ridges, slopes, and canyon bottoms. Where the landforms didn't connect—where the route crosses a canyon, as it does just before it drops into Malibu—engineers added fill or blasted through rock to create the three tunnels that carry the road through the heart of the Santa Monica Mountains. When Malibu incorporated, antisewer alumni and newly elected city council members Walt Keller and Carolyn Van Horn were among those who argued that Los Angeles County should be responsible for the two-mile section of Kanan Dume Road that falls within Malibu's city limits, as the state is responsible for Pacific Coast Highway. There was also the consideration that Kanan Dume wasn't the only highway the county had built in these mountains. Besides Malibu Canyon Road, there are three other cross-mountain routes, all with a history of problems: Latigo Canyon Road, Tuna Canyon Road, and Las Flores Canyon Road, where I watched the steam shovel operator attempt to stop Las Flores Creek from overflowing its banks. Perhaps the incorporation organizers had reviewed maintenance figures from the county's public works department showing that in a routine year Malibu should be prepared to spend as much as a quarter of its annual budget on its roads. Perhaps by insisting the county should be responsible for Kanan Dume Road, Keller–Van Horn et al. were seeking to avert a fiscal crisis for our new government. But Los Angeles County grasped the implications immediately. The board of supervisors wasted no time introducing a bill in the California legislature that *forced* Malibu to *take* Kanan Dume Road, as Keller–Van Horn put it.

I first heard there were problems with Kanan Dume Road when Councilman Keller questioned an expenditure of $100,000 submitted for approval by the public works director. The request covered the cost of a temporary repair on a section of the highway that had failed. Keller called for a complete investigation. Hadn't the public works director acted on his own initiative, proceeding with the repair without first seeking council approval (a major infraction in the Keller manual of civic procedure), and wasn't this Kanan Dume Road after all? Salt on the wounds.

The public works director explained that the repair was necessary to tie the roadbed together and keep the asphalt from breaking up with a landslide that had recently been activated. But by the time he made his next appearance before the council, he was forced to admit the unauthorized repair had failed. The difficulty was that the section of road in question had been built atop 100 feet of fill, to which the county had subsequently applied three layers of asphalt patches in an attempt to keep the surface from cracking. Adding fuel to the fire, the public works director explained that he had moved quickly to take advantage of "a window of opportunity" wherein the county itself closed Kanan Dume Road to repair a slide in its jurisdiction. He said that the idea for Malibu's repair was to hold together the section of road the city was responsible for long enough to get through the winter rainy season and perhaps the following summer's beach traffic. Then what? The man in charge of Malibu's infrastructure offered no hint of what his next move might be if the repairs managed to hold the road together, and the council members asked no further questions.

None of this should have come as a surprise. More than two hundred landslides have been mapped in the foothills and canyons on which Malibu's homes and highways are built, and at one time or another most of us have experienced the consequences—rocks on the road, detours, someone's deck skidding into your backyard—and although many of Malibu's slides are described as ancient (no one knows when they moved last), many others are active and likely to give way if wind or water dislodges boulders or an earthquake activates an underlying fault. (In 1994, the Northridge earthquake, centered on a shallow fault north of Malibu, triggered fourteen hundred landslides in the Santa Monica Mountains.) In Malibu's expansive clay soils, water is often the culprit. Moisture infiltrates unstable soil and causes particles to roll along each other like BBS until gravity forces the whole mass downhill. Thus did the public works director diagnose that a drain for a private home built uphill from Kanan Dume Road disturbed the natural drainage in the area and caused an existing slide to begin moving.

"That's why we didn't want to take the road in the first place," Councilwoman Van Horn reminded the city council. "We knew there were problems with the engineering."

With nothing on the downhill side to contain it—no railroad ties, no interlocking concrete blocks or steel girders—the Kanan Dume slide kept moving, nine inches in one month. Unable to predict when a sudden jerk or twitch might shear off the road's downcanyon lanes, the city engineer restriped the highway from four lanes to two, temporarily shifting traffic away from the slide. The city manager reported that this temporary detour would remain in place indefinitely: "On the list of bad outcomes, the slide could continue to move and the whole road could go."

The public works director offered more bad news: he estimated the cost to contain the slide and repair the road at just under half a million dollars. But much of Malibu's financial reserve was leveraged against reimbursements the city expected from FEMA for past disasters. At least, said the public works director, give me enough money to determine what the problem is and what we can do about it.

The council members said they preferred to wait and see. But wait and see what? Did they expect Los Angeles County would suddenly acknowledge the road it had secured a state law to divest itself of, or that

FEMA would give the wheels of the federal government a kick and someone would rush to cut Malibu a check? Eventually I came to understand that wait-and-see is typical of situations that don't lend themselves to easy resolution. "Wait-and-see" precedes even the sidestep of studying a problem. When community leaders decide to wait and see, it likely means they have yet to identify a culprit or the political ramifications of the situation haven't revealed themselves. Possibly intervening circumstances will arise that will deflect attention from the problem—or best of all, if they wait the situation will somehow resolve itself.

Until the slide threatened traffic on Kanan Dume Road, it never occurred to me that I lived in the Santa Monica Mountains. Mountains to me were the Adirondacks of my childhood. Mountains meant vacation, a place to visit. Driving along PCH at the base of Malibu's foothills I never thought of myself as being in the mountains. When I traveled through Malibu Canyon on my way to a movie or a meal in the San Fernando Valley, I might acknowledge the scenery, but I was not in touch with the fact that living in Malibu, I was living in the mountains as surely as if I had pitched a tent three thousand feet up Sandstone Peak. This was in spite of the fact that the mountains routinely end up in Malibu's backyard and their slopes of poorly cemented sedimentary rock regularly block passage around town. In the same manner it had completely slipped by me that the area drained by the creek that bears Malibu's name is the mountains' largest watershed and the creek itself is the only stream that runs completely through the width of the range.

In Malibu we live in the wildest part of the Santa Monica Mountains. Here the landscape is least developed, the land most open, the populations of wildlife most abundant. Anyone who takes refuge in Malibu keeps company with coyotes and quail, mule deer and bobcats, and with luck, now and then a cougar. But with development pushing farther and farther into this wild land, how long this can last is anybody's guess. On the surface, Malibu Canyon Road links the San Fernando Valley with Malibu's sand, but the canyon the highway runs through is part of one of only two corridors that tie together the islands of habitat the mountains' large predators depend on to survive. Cougars and bobcats and coyotes know nothing of our human jurisdictions—over the mountains from Malibu, north through the Conejo Valley the big cats move, then through the Simi Hills and still farther north to the Los Padres National Forest, twenty, thirty miles as the crow flies. There is no such thing as a Malibu cougar any more than Malibu Creek belongs to those of us who live in Malibu. But both the cougars and the creek are vital to what draws us here, no matter how seldom we might think about them.

I left the city with a dream of a child-size portion of ground to call my own. The gift of the acre of land I settled on was to lead me footstep by footstep toward a more realistic understanding of the landscape I had chosen. With the cougars I roamed north from Point Dume up the heavily forested mountain foothills into the mountains themselves, then down into the dry valley on the other side, until I understood that each of these places is functionally related to the other: the mountains' heavy bulk captures the ocean moisture that keeps their southwestern slopes thick with toyon and oak, vegetation that gives way at the crest to grasses and sage where the soil is thinner and less nurturing. Here ground squirrels are more prevalent, as are the rattlesnakes and raptors that prey on them.

The degree to which we urban expatriates don't understand the relationships that keep this resource we occupy vital surfaced in a conversation with Councilwoman Joan House. When I wondered about her vision for the community, House told me people in Malibu want a place that's "relaxed, friendly, and laid back." And "if you build a town to serve visitors, you're going to have a sea of asphalt and a lot of empty buildings you have to service and take care of." As if, with the mountains at our back and the ocean at our front door, people come here to sit in a darkened movie theater or shop.

As the council members mulled over allocating funds to study the slide that threatened Kanan Dume Road, residents who live along Tuna Canyon Road appeared in the council chambers to demand repair of a landslide that narrowed their road from two lanes to one. Close on their heels came residents along Latigo Canyon Road, five minutes from the Kanan Dume slide, to protest a threefold increase in an assessment levied for de-watering wells that stabilized a slide endangering their canyon roadway. Third in line were residents from the Las Flores Canyon area who worried that three active slides threatened their only way in and out and who wanted the city council to develop an emergency evacuation route.

The council members listened carefully to each of these requests, as they had listened to the public works director's request for funds to evaluate the slide that threatened to close Kanan Dume Road, but decided to refer each to the staff for study. Eventually residents of Tuna Canyon Road were dismissed on the rationale that since they lived outside Malibu city limits, the council had no jurisdiction over their problem. Likewise, plans for the Las Flores Canyon escape route bogged down in discussions of possible alternatives and relative costs. Only the Latigo Canyon Road residents persisted until the city council finally voted to abolish their assessment district. But what it gave with one hand the council took away with the other, refusing to allocate funds to replace the lost income. This left residents with the Catch 22 of additional change in their pockets but a greater risk their road would slide.

All the while the Kanan Dume slide continued to move. By the time the council approved the funds to study what it would take to repair the road, the slide was seventy-five feet wide at the roadbed and had expanded to a width of three hundred feet as it moved down the canyon, causing council members to fret that Malibu would be liable should motorists find themselves in the wrong place on the road at the wrong time. "If we think the road is compromised," said the city engineer, "we'll close it."

Close it? With Kanan Dume closed, the community would be left with one north-south route over the mountains—one way in for firefighting companies, one way out for paramedics delivering patients to hospitals in the Valley. "We could have one or two Kanan Roads in an unlucky year," the city geologist told the council, but by now, Keller and Van Horn had found their footing. The two antidevelopment council members insisted their constituents preferred the road remain the way it was if repairing it meant Malibu had to ante up. It was a matter of principle: the county built the road, the county gets the problems. But Los Angeles County stood its ground. It was itself undergoing a major shortfall of funds. "Nobody has any money," the public works director told the city council. By that time, the Kanan Dume slide had been moving for almost a year.

As the council dithered, nature, which had always had the upper hand, made its move. On a pleasant day in late September, with the sun pushing temperatures into the high seventies and housewives from the San Fernando Valley sneaking over the mountains for one last day at the beach, the slide under Kanan Dume Road gave a final push, like a woman giving birth, and sent the two northbound lanes of the highway thirty feet into the canyon below. With the consequences of its dithering now evident, it seemed only logical that the council would finally act. But slowly what had been unthinkable a year ago began to settle in. Public works crews blocked the failed section of highway with concrete barricades and installed a locked gate on the uphill shoulder, the only remaining section of the road the city engineer considered safe. Sheriff's deputies and fire department paramedics were issued keys that allowed them emergency access to the shoulder route, but as fast as crews installed locks on the gate, exasperated residents cut them off. One enterprising citizen drove a bulldozer two miles up from Pacific Coast Highway and tried unsuccessfully to push aside the concrete barriers. Only motorcyclists made it through, wearing a path in the narrow space between the slide and the locked gate.

"A lot of people didn't believe this was a problem because a lot of people didn't believe the road wouldn't be fixed by now," the owner of a restaurant and convention center north of the closed road told the city council. "We need your leadership to draw out our potential."

Through it all, the slide moved, on one occasion four and a half feet in three days. Then cracks began to appear in the shoulder, threatening the fire department's emergency route. A year after he had first alerted council members to the problem with Kanan Dume Road, and with another rainy season setting in, the public works director again asked for funds, this time to protect residents whose homes were in the path of the slide. A shift in its movement had crushed the pipe that drained the fill the road was built on, and he feared that heavy rains expected during the upcoming El Niño winter would send a sea of mud down the canyon and into backyards at the bottom. With a gaping thirty-foot-deep hole where four lanes of traffic once passed, the price tag to repair the slide and open the road had doubled to just over a million dollars.

Communities like Malibu that have little commercial or industrial base typically rely on three sources of revenue: property taxes, sales tax, and a tax on utilities such as telephone and electricity to deliver both basic services and any peculiar amenities residents consider important. In Malibu, sales tax is third behind county property taxes and the utility tax. In contrast, sales tax is the primary source of funds for Calabasas, our neighbor across the mountains, where three automobile dealerships generate a large chunk of income. The remainder of the budget for both towns comes from countywide bond issues and state-mandated tariffs such as the vehicle gas tax, plus any federal money we're eligible for.

"A community incorporates for a reason," says Calabasas' former planning director. "To have a larger say in decision-making or to create an identity on a local level. The difficulty is that more and more what a community wants, it must pay for itself."

Calabasas councilman Dennis Washburn observes that both county and state governments have become increasingly less generous in sharing money with communities like ours. (Calabasas retains a little over 3 percent of the property taxes Los Angeles County collects from its residents, Malibu 6.5 percent.) "Our vision," says Washburn, "is to promote the long-term viability of our community in the face of some massive movements to curtail local government's ability to sustain itself."

Local government has been further crippled by a recent run of statewide initiatives that give voters a direct say in how they're taxed. Decisions that were once the prerogative of elected officials now require a vote of the populace. But the news isn't as good as it sounds. When residents of Agoura Hills, a community of 19,000 just west of Calabasas, voted out their utility tax, they were left with only one alternative to replace lost revenue. But increasing sales tax and other service-related revenue requires more development, precisely what many Agoura Hills residents—like their neighbors in Calabasas and Malibu—moved to the community to escape.

Councilman Washburn is emphatic. "The president and Congress do nothing for me. They don't sweep our streets. They don't build our parks. They might give us some money. But we have to be organized to get it."

So money determines the degree to which a community controls its own destiny? And to live the way residents prefer, a community must cooperate with large and powerful outside agencies that may not appear to have the community's best interests at heart? "What you need a government for is to negotiate with other government agencies to strike deals," says former Malibu planning director Bob Benard.

But if negotiations fail, or as seems to be the case in Malibu, if negotiations are dismissed out of hand?

"The community has to belly up."

"I can't believe you deliberated for four and a half hours and didn't allow time to set goals for the repair of Kanan Dume Road." Planning Commissioner Barbara Cameron glared at the five city council members sitting at the front of the city hall conference room where they had called a special meeting to discuss Malibu's infrastructure. "This was not an appropriate message to send to the people of this community." What, I wondered, was Cameron thinking? From what I had seen at council meetings, from the messages I'd retrieved off my answering machine and letters to the editor in both newspapers, the community didn't seem much troubled by the closure of Kanan Dume Road or the slim prospects for its repair. The public works director tells me that based on the calls he's received at city hall, most of the people who have bothered to register an opinion are in favor of keeping the road closed. As if to prove the point, a proclosure resident appeared at a recent city council meeting with a chart she insisted established that more out-of-towners than Malibu residents use Kanan Dume Road—more than enough reason that Malibu shouldn't foot the bill for the road's repair. There was also Councilman Walt Keller's suggestion that Malibu should rebuild Kanan Dume as a toll road: anyone who wants to visit has to pay. When this idea fizzled, Keller insisted Malibu follow Los Angeles County and take its case to the state legislature. Next to him on the dais, Councilwoman Van Horn worried about allocating a disproportionate share of community resources to one problem.

Listening to this bickering, I wondered what audience the two council members thought they were playing to. Did they really believe the county should fix the road? (Councilwoman House had yet to weigh in on the issue, appearing to test which way the wind would ultimately blow, and so far property-rights activist Harlow appeared to be neutral.) There was also the question of what would happen if Malibu actually had the money to fix the road. How would the votes fall then? Councilwoman Van Horn reminds us that if a slide blocked Pacific Coast Highway twenty years ago, residents hitched up their belts and drove north for twenty miles, then backtracked forty miles south to Santa Monica. But twenty years ago the community was smaller and we lacked a government to look after our welfare.

Finally, there was Councilman Keller's observation, which he appeared to take as justification for the city's lack of action in the matter of Kanan Dume Road. "People in Malibu," Keller advised his fellow council members, "just want to be left alone."

Like many others, I have discovered opportunity in this crisis. The concrete barriers that block traffic at either end of the Kanan Dume slide have created a pocket park. People like me, who didn't know this part of the mountains before the county pushed its road through, have a chance for discovery. I walk the dogs on the closed stretch of highway, other people bring their horses or ride mountain bikes. With so many of the old trails blocked, we are happy to have a place to move about. I kick a ball up the empty asphalt, and the dogs chase it, zigzagging across lanes, dodging rocks and tree branches that have accumulated since crews from both Malibu and the county abandoned this stretch of highway. North of the slide, the public works director is stockpiling dirt for the day the city council presents him the money to fix the road. The dogs and I climb these dirt mounds like Lilliputians over Gulliver. High above the road, I listen to the sound of a stream I didn't know was there; with the dogs, I cock my ear to the muffled calls of quail feeding in the underbrush. Off to the south a necklace of shoreline lights brightens from Santa Monica to Marina del Rey to Palos Verdes, throwing off a yellow glow that defuses slowly into the encroaching dark.

For three months the dogs and I have climbed these piles. I hold their leashes tight as the heavy tandem dump trucks trundle past, driving north. One by one the trucks lumber onto the steep piles, open their bottoms, then flatten their cone-shaped deposits. When the dirt becomes too high to drive across, the first in another line of trucks begins another pile. One of the dogs uncovers a broken branch among the pieces of tires and crushed soda cans that litter the mounds as they snake farther and farther north from the slide. We move along on our high mounds like desert travelers on a knife-edged ridge of sand. High above the highway, I consider the possibilities if Kanan Dume Road were to be permanently closed. With the road closed, there would be no noise up here on the ridge and no car exhaust. Those of us who live at this far end of Malibu would be relieved of the tension of people coming and going. We would have the neighborhood to ourselves again.

Standing above the road, I allow the darkening sky to still my thoughts. A long, slow tug of innocence pulls me back, until I am sitting again at Hana's table, a glass of wine at my elbow. Tonight I sit at the foot of the table, watching the sundown sky out Hana's picture window. In another ten minutes, when the light is completely gone, some of us will decamp to the hot tub on the deck, where we will forgo wine and conversation and count the stars as they rise.

Standing on the ridge, buffeted by the cool night air, once again I sense the feeling of being suspended beyond ordinary circumstances, perched on the edge of a future I was sure would be so much better than the past. Seconds float by, minutes. Suddenly I hate this road and the county for building it. I hate the tire noise and the roar of downshifting engines, the squeal of brakes on tight curves, the surfers from the Valley who multiply each year and strut Malibu's sand as if they own it, the gangs who appear tugging at pit bulls in spiked collars. I hate that sheriff's deputies now patrol the beach wearing guns.

The sun makes its final drop into the ink-dark sea, leaving behind a chill so sharp it snaps me from my reverie. I turn away from the ocean and lead the dogs back across the mounds of dirt. I settle for the thought that it has been good to have a chance to see what this canyon was like before Los Angeles County built its road, as Hana's daughter described it being thirty years ago, when she snuck off to walk here with her boyfriend to go exploring.

On a day when a solution to the problem of Kanan Dume Road seemed most out of reach, seventy people appeared to demonstrate at the slide. This tentative effort at citizen initiative was not organized by angry mothers who couldn't get their kids to school or off-duty paramedics concerned about the time it took to deliver patients to the hospital. No, this first effort at civic responsibility was arranged by the businessman whose restaurant and convention center had been cut off at the far side of the slide. He was joined by a spattering of Malibu residents, a group of real estate agents fed up with the closed road, and homeowners who lived nearby. The director of the chamber of commerce confirmed what other restaurant owners and businessmen in Malibu already knew: with the road closed, business in Malibu was down as much as 50 percent, and sales tax income, the town's third largest source of revenue, had dropped in proportion. In a show of solidarity, the demonstrators were photographed standing in front of the slide. Ten minutes later the ground they had stood on dropped into the canyon.

Still the city council dithered. "You can't have it both ways," Zev Yaroslavsky, Malibu's representative on the Los Angeles County Board of Supervisors, warned us. "Your town is responsible for its infrastructure." The supervisor suggested a community-wide benefit-assessment district similar to what other communities he represents had developed to provide civic improvements. But the majority of Malibu's city council members had been among incorporation organizers and had promised no new taxes. There would be no assessment district.

The stalemate continued until the position of mayor, which rotates among council members, was handed off to Jeff Jennings. "I agree with everybody in town and everybody on this council who says we shouldn't shoulder this burden alone," the new mayor told his colleagues. "But we can be right until hell freezes over and it won't get the road fixed."

As the mayor was sworn in, an organization calling itself Residents to Re-Open Kanan—ROK—gathered to demonstrate at the slide. One of the organizers, a real estate agent who had lived through much of the same history Councilwoman Van Horn laid claim to, bent my ear with possibilities the group was considering, from bake sales to canvassing Malibu's celebrities for money to repair the road. Why not, I suggested, act like grown-ups?

So it was that after one or two false starts, petitions began appearing around town demanding the city council find a way to open Kanan Dume Road; faxes supporting Supervisor Yaroslavsky's position that the town must step up to the plate clogged the telephone lines at the Hall of Administration in downtown Los Angeles. At the same time, ROK members kept up a dogged vigil at city council meetings. Nor was there any grass growing under the new mayor's feet. Within weeks of his inauguration, Mayor Jennings and Supervisor Yaroslavsky met to "kick some ideas around." Negotiations continued, and within weeks the city council had an agreement to consider: the county would lend Malibu the money to fix Kanan Dume Road, provided the loan was secured by the town's state transportation and gas tax allotments. The county would pave the way for Malibu to redeem the money (and take a commission for the service), and once the deal was approved, Supervisor Yaroslavsky would commit $88,000 from his discretionary fund to help fix the slide and open the road.

Councilman Keller joined Councilwoman Van Horn to argue against committing such a large amount of the city's entitlements to one project, while John Harlow took issue with the amount of the county's commission, leaving Councilwoman House to vote with Mayor Jennings now that a constructive solution had presented itself. The woman with the chart reappeared at city council meetings, but Supervisor Yaroslavsky was adamant. "Should residents of Malibu who use the roads in Beverly Hills pay to repair the roads in Beverly Hills?" When he ran out of reasons to object to the solution the mayor and the supervisor had negotiated, Keller called for a survey. Residents could take their pick: put all the money on Kanan Dume Road, distribute the funds throughout town, or hoard it. When Van Horn supported the survey, it was too much for one ROK organizer, who sprinted to the microphone with a folder of petitions and faxes favoring the loan from the county. "Here's your survey."

"We've already had a survey," said Mayor Jennings. "It's called an election."

Similar to the way pulling weeds during the quiet summer I spent with Doris Hoover helped me appreciate the nature of the environment in which I had settled, the controversy surrounding the repair of Kanan Dume Road prompted me to reconsider Malibu's relationships outside the community. I had never given much thought to the idea that we might work with Los Angeles County—or that we had obligations beyond ourselves. I had absorbed the common wisdom that our relationship with the county was bound to be antagonistic and we had enough on our plate to worry about anyone else.

An action causes a reaction, which causes some other event to occur, then another, until you find yourself squarely up against the limits of your control. As long as we stood firm in our position that the county should repair Kanan Dume Road, we were powerless to affect a solution to our problem. By the same token, the action Malibu mayor Jennings took when he met with Los Angeles County supervisor Yaroslavsky triggered a series of positive reactions: the mayor's outreach to the supervisor opened a dialogue that led to brainstorming, then negotiations that culminated in the county's assistance in resolving Malibu's difficulty. Energy released at the head of the system transformed itself constructively in a manner similar to the way energy from the sun is transformed in the presence of water and nourishment to produce the pleasant scent of a flower or a tree that provides us shade. But to be useful this energy must flow.

I went to Malibu to isolate, but no matter how small the territory I tried to pace off for myself, I was never able to anticipate all the factors that might disturb the neat and predictable world I imagined. But to be part of even something small, one must appreciate the larger picture. How could we fail to recognize that the Kanan Dume slide and the Latigo Canyon slide and the slides above Las Flores Canyon were related? That a similar natural dynamic underlies all three and is a fixture of this mountain landscape we have chosen to inhabit? When I lived in the city, I felt buffeted by forces beyond my control. I longed for a piece of ground I could preside over exclusively. I had lost touch with what my father had confided to me in those other mountains in upstate New York so many years before: that each one of us, whether individual or community or an entire society, develops toward maturity in the same manner as the natural life that surrounds us, by taking in sustenance and putting forth energy toward the well-being of the whole.

The Malibu City Council finally approved the deal with Los Angeles County to fix Kanan Dume Road. The public works director put the project out to bid, and just one month short of the upcoming city council election, Mayor Jennings, flanked by the founders of ROK, cut a flower-decked ribbon and reopened the road. The convention center owner who laid the foundation for ROK's support of the mayor's compromise with the county brought a catering truck to the reopening ceremony and offered free lunch to celebrants. Speeches were made by ROK and representatives from the county; a spokesman for the California Highway Patrol explained plans for traffic enforcement now that the road was open. Mayor Jennings and his wife were persuaded to mount horses and have their photograph taken. Standing in the warm spring sun, Willie Nelson blaring from the catering truck, it seemed Malibu might be entering a new era; perhaps we had finally conquered the post-incorporation jitters.

ROK had a sign made thanking Mayor Jennings and Supervisor Yaroslavsky and placed it close to where the slide had dropped into the canyon, so everyone who drove by could read it, the commuters from Camarillo, the beachgoers from the San Fernando Valley, Malibu residents driving over the mountains to shop in the valley's malls. A month after the sign was installed, Malibu held its third city council election. With only a third of registered voters bothering to go to the polls, we voted the man who initiated the compromise with Los Angeles County out of office.

So there it was again, the falling back, the inclination to cut and run, just when it appeared the higher ground might be taken.

Long Way Home

Public life can only be reclaimed by understanding, and then practicing, its connection to real, identifiable places.

Daniel Kemmis, *Community and the Politics of Place*

1999

In the photograph I see Lee Washington sitting in the middle of the gold sofa that runs along the far wall of the basket room in her house in Zuma Canyon. I remember that I moved a few steps backward into the living room to take the picture, so the doorway between the two rooms frames Lee sitting on the couch alone.

A glass display case hangs on the wall above where Lee is sitting, and behind the case and the sofa, fabric that looks like wet straw reflects thin, honeyed strands of light onto the surface of Lee's baskets. The baskets are everywhere, in the cabinet above the sofa, on an old-fashioned maple end table, in a bookcase at the far end of the room, on the floor, on throw rugs that cover the brick-colored linoleum. A woman behind me asks how many baskets are collected in this room, and Lee says she figures perhaps a thousand. Most were woven by California women, but some come from as far away as the Great Plains. Lee reminds the woman that this room used to be Michael's gun room. Michael is Lee's husband, and he has been dead for almost four years.

The image of Lee Washington sitting alone with her baskets has drawn me away from the living room full of talking, laughing people. The golden glow off the walls and the baskets and the light filtering through the straw-colored shades on the long-necked lamps at either end of the sofa draw Lee farther back into the room, into a warm cave of encapsulated time that blends her image with the ghosts of the women whose work surrounds her. She sits there, handmaiden to this exhibit of primitive artistry yet anchored to this house and its modern past.

Old friends Bill Hublein and Larry Franklin sit drinking wine on an overstuffed sofa in Lee's living room. Larry's wife, Kate, stands with a group of women near the bay window at the far end of the room, where they critique Lee's Christmas tree, which this year is decorated with angels. One woman explains to the others why Lee wanted angels on her tree this year, and each compares this angel tree with trees from Christmases past. Bob Barret sits in a corner easy chair watching his wife, Barbara, take pictures of me taking pictures.

Coming up the long driveway to Lee Washington's house with Kate and Larry, I had heard Kate once again mark the years as she always does when we gather here, by the twelve-foot bushes that run along the front of Lee's property. Kate remembers when the trees were a three-foot hedge. In the living room, another woman recalls Lee's antiques sale from last year or the year before, and someone else her long-running Easter egg hunt, staged these days for the children of the original egg gatherers. Across the hall in the dining room, Kate and Bill Hublein's wife, Natalie, have discovered some new bowl or lamp or table they hadn't noticed the last time they were here. Lee's daughter is also with us tonight with her family. She recalls past Christmases or Easters or birthdays the older women remember in their own way.

Friend Janie Hall lived across the street from Kate and Larry until she moved to the east end of town after she and her husband divorced. This is Janie's first Christmas in her new home. Three years ago she lost everything when the Old Topanga fire roared through her neighborhood. For two years she lived in a trailer on her burned-out property, marking the progress as her son rebuilt her house.

Lee Washington's home breathes with these memories. Forty years of births and then birthdays, of seeing children fall in love and marry, of mourning friends who have died and missing those who have moved away. Bill Hublein rode with Lee's husband on the sheriff's mounted posse. In the sixties they rousted half-naked flower children from the willows along Malibu Creek. Bill and Natalie ran the community's first plumbing service, then passed it on to their son; in her spare time, Natalie sold horse tack out of the garage. In three weeks Betty North will call to tell me her twenty-year-old son has been asked to ride on the neighborhood Christmas float as he did as a child. Santa visits Point Dume every Christmas Eve, riding on a makeshift float of lights and music and calling for children to confide last-minute wishes before he begins his sleigh-drawn rounds. Last year a county fire engine pulled the float, and Kate Franklin's son and daughter-in-law photographed the kids with Santa.

I met Betty North on a Saturday afternoon drinking wine at Hana's table. She was speaking of the man she was dating; he was ill and she feared the loss of the relationship. I have followed the progress of Janie Hall's new house as each small step has been completed, and although I have never met Janie's daughter, who lives north up the coast, I have admired photographs of her new quarterhorse and her dog, which I recognize as an Australian shepherd. I have seen photographs of Lee Washington dressed in high-waisted pants, bolero jacket, and flat-topped Spanish hat, leading her daughter on a pony in a horseshow arena. I can't see from the photograph, but I would bet the line behind Lee includes one of Bill and Natalie's daughters and Kate's daughter, Kelly. I have in my own house a photograph of Bob Barret sitting on my couch next to Kate's husband. Bob looks as much at home as when he owned the place, before he sold it to a friend, who sold it to me. The Barrets' old acre backs up to Kate Franklin's property, and the two families tore down their fences to build a ring for their children to train their horses.

I don't have a picture of Kate and Larry's wedding, when they married after almost twenty years living together, but in my mind the images are keen: The bride almost an hour late, the minister pacing. Kate's son in a tuxedo riding to the wedding on his Harley-Davidson. Rick Bentley, a woodworker who paneled my living room, tending bar. His wife, Susan, worked the dining room crew and discovered the coffee cups hadn't been delivered. We called the restaurant down the beach. A hundred cups? No problem. Send them back clean.

I see other images of this interweaving among the fabrics of one another's lives. I see Arnold York, the publisher of *The Malibu Times,* balancing a load of steaks and lobsters in Hughes Supermarket, supplies for his homeowners association's annual summer barbecue. I see residents standing in line outside the market to buy yet another losing ticket in the raffle that every year kicks off the Kiwanis Club's annual Chili Cook-off, when the whole town comes out to eat chili and pancakes, ride the Ferris wheel, and listen to rock music. In earlier years, part of the excitement was guessing what hat actor Larry Hagman would wear as MC.

The magazine articles that seek to understand what we're looking for in places where we attempt to make our homes insist that we have had enough of traffic congestion and crime, that we want better schools and less crowded public facilities and an end to feelings of rootlessness. We want a slower pace, and we yearn for a "genuine sense of community." When pressed, we speak of wanting to know our neighbors, of being able to walk to the store or the park or the movie theater. Most of all, we yearn for the rewards of face-to-face communication. We speak of wanting more quality in our lives, of spending less time going to and from work. We want more time with our families. More time at home.

Planners and developers who attempt to interpret these longings talk about new perspectives on small-town living. They seem to think we want to live together in friendly association, in fellowship that emphasizes our mutuality. Among the places they have designed to fulfill these longings, Seaside, on Florida's Gulf Coast, was one of the first, a model village where architectural standards impose a physical plan designed to suggest the interactive patterns we associate with small-town living. Houses in Seaside have porches because porches provide an opening in the facade that fronts on the street and suggest welcome and accessibility. From their porches, residents can wave hello to neighbors. In Seaside, roads circle and loop rather than being laid out in a grid. Commercial areas are designed so residents can shop close to home.

In California, planner Peter Calthorpe has pinned his hopes on light rail as an antidote to the state's automobile culture. Calthorpe designed Laguna West in northern Sacramento County on a pedestrian scale, and closer to home the Malibu Bay Company hired the futurist to develop a plan for the property it owns in the civic center. But Malibu leaders dismissed the project as too dense, apparently without considering that a compromise might be effected—or the value of having a planner of Calthorpe's stature onboard.

But the perfect layout is not enough. Release from crowding and crime and too much traffic is not enough. The easy commute to work or school or shopping is not enough. People must want to live together. Otherwise they run the risk of what haunts us here. Established in our secluded setting, at home in this "right" place, we wall ourselves in; we avoid experiences that might enlarge our sense of who we are and what we're doing here. We deprive ourselves of lifeblood.

Another snapshot: This time I am alone in the back seat of a rented limousine on my way home to Malibu from Los Angeles International Airport. I am hurt, I am angry, and I am tired. Tears slide down my face and onto my hands, which are folded tightly in my lap. Two hours earlier I was in this same limousine going in the opposite direction, and where I now sit alone a man and his wife and their six-year-old son smiled across from me. The boy was blond like his father, who was tall and uncomfortable with nowhere to put his legs. The boy sat perched on the edge of the seat between his parents, as if his enthusiasm could make the limousine go faster. His mother held a bouquet of roses. A long-sought dream was about to unfold.

It was Hana's daughter, Jennifer, who sat across from me with her husband and their son. The boy held a small backpack full of games and books for this trip that would take the family first to Honolulu, then to Lihue, Kauai. Except for the boy, we had all been together in a limousine like this once before, although there were more of us and I was still living in my house near Beverly Hills. We had been on our way to dinner and a show at the Magic Castle that night to celebrate that Hana was in town with her new beau, but the driver got lost and we drove around Hollywood for an hour drinking scotch and listening to Hawaiian music.

Hana's son was the first to leave Malibu; he went to the Big Island first, then to Kauai, where Hana followed. Three years later Jennifer was married in the stone church across the street from her mother's new house on Kauai's north shore. Two months later Hana hosted a luau for her daughter and new son-in-law at the beach club down from Trancas Field. Then Hana went back to Hawaii for good, and Jennifer and her husband set themselves up in her old house in Malibu, where on some days there still wasn't enough water and the regulars still gathered to drink wine.

I stood at the curb at the airport that gray morning in July, watching the limousine driver unload luggage and Hana's grandson pull at his mother's skirt, anxious to be off. I know I hugged each one of them and waved goodbye and said things like "Have a good trip" and "See you soon," and then they were gone. Struggling to keep a brave face, I thought of two years before, when Hana came home for Christmas and we all chipped in and hired a chauffeured Lincoln Continental. I went with the driver to the airport while the rest of regulars waited at home, Jennifer and her husband and the neighbors from next door and across the street, the kind of homecoming that makes you want to pull out the flannel pajamas. Now I am sitting in the backseat of this limousine by myself. The other table regulars have gone about their business, finding solace in routine, but my day has a bigger hole in it. I have seen it firsthand: they are gone, first Hana, now her daughter. Now Hana is really gone. There will be no more last-minute phone calls the week before Christmas: Mom's coming home. Mom's coming with her new boyfriend, and they're bringing their friend so-and-so. Now there is no place for Hana to come to. I was in my rented house when Hana's boyfriend and the policeman from Honolulu brought out their guitars and we all sang "Hanalei Moon" on New Year's Eve, and I was living in my own house, I'm sure, when Hana's daughter called me to come to dinner and meet her father.

I used to wait for those phone calls; dinner stretched into entire evenings away from my aloneness. First it was Jennifer and her husband and I, then the carpenter who lived in the guesthouse, then Kate from across the street. When Jennifer and her husband went to Hawaii for two weeks before they left for good, I took care of the garden. I culled extra tomatoes, picked piles of green beans and zucchini so the vegetables wouldn't rot on the vine. In my mind I was pulling an oar in both our lives. Now they are all gone. How will I pass that house every day knowing I will never again watch a sunset out Hana's picture window?

"I knew I would leave when the mesa got built," Jennifer told me one afternoon in our wine-drinking. She meant the piece of land at the corner, where Pacific Coast Highway drops away from Point Dume toward Zuma Beach. She exaggerated—the buildings weren't really on the mesa, but they were close enough and they were ugly and it was time to go, time to find another place where young girls could decorate their pony carts at Easter and drive them around the neighborhood and three-year-olds could wander across the street and the woman next door would bring them home. Time to find a place where mothers aren't frightened by the homeless men who live by the creek. In her kitchen in Hawaii, Hana keeps a photograph of a restaurant in west Malibu, just the one building by itself, so alone it could be in west Texas. Today the cookie-cutter subdivision winds down the ridge behind where the restaurant used to be; next door there's a supermarket, and soon there'll be condominiums across the street in Trancas Field. In Hana's mind, the skeleton in that photograph was reason enough to leave, the death knell for her version of Malibu's way of life.

Much is different now from the years when I spent weekends driving out to Hana's. There are streetlights on Pacific Coast Highway near the center of town and the big pink shopping center where the old Colony market used to be, appealing enough except for the bright lights and the asphalt parking lot in front of the stores. Farther out, houses cling to ridges that once fell uninterrupted to the coast, and on Point Dume fences and walls and tennis courts block what is left of the horse trails we once rode. I get a ticket now if I walk my dogs on the beach.

When the professionals the city council hired to plan our civic center asked Malibu residents what we like most about where we live, we described the slow pace and the "vacation feel" of the community, the sense of safety, the lack of crime, and the access to Los Angeles combined with Malibu's small-town atmosphere. We spoke of the ocean and beaches, the climate and the clean air, our access to nature and wildlife, and Malibu's rural character. We were less sanguine about traffic, and we complained there wasn't enough parking. Some among us were upset that the town lacked a center and that they have to leave Malibu to shop. No one worried about not having enough privacy, a complaint frequently heard in cities, although some of us were concerned about what we described as hostility among neighbors.

It has been more than two years since homeowners met with property owners to plan the civic center. The planning commission rehashed much of what the Civic Center Specific Plan Advisory Committee had worked out in detail, and the Malibu Coalition for Slow Growth countered the professionals' plan with a version of its own. If the planning commission's revisions are ratified by the city council, there is no possibility Joan Knapp will be able to build her senior-living complex and no chance for a community hospital. Harry Barovsky, vice chair of the planning commission, whose wife, Sharon, put so much effort into the advisory committee, led a move to strip property owners of development bonuses they might receive if they donated land toward the civic center's infrastructure. Barovsky took the view that the community would have no need for a wastewater treatment plant if the civic center weren't developed. Taken to its logical extreme, this would mean the town wouldn't be obligated to provide public infrastructure—roads and storm drains and traffic lights—if the purpose was to support development. As if shops and restaurants and a children's museum would be of no benefit to the community. (Was this, perhaps, Malibu's version of the conventional developers' agreement, wherein the right to build is exchanged for something the community needs like a park or a new downtown intersection?) Another planning commissioner rejected the consultants' plan entirely, calling it "too visitor serving."

The planning commission also recommended that any wastewater effluent from the sewage treatment plant proposed for Joan Knapp's property would have to be sterilized, an additional process that would be costly, and while it would allow for expanded use of reclaimed water, the idea seemed designed more as another hoop for property owners to jump through. Further complicating the situation, some among the planning commissioners suggested that a self-contained wastewater treatment plant might not be the most logical solution to the area's sewage problems and recommended businesses be allowed to use septic tanks.

Thus have some things changed and many others not. The restaurants, banks, and beauty parlors in the civic center are still cycling their wastewater through septic systems, and many in Malibu still blame the Las Virgenes Municipal Water District's water reclamation facility upstream in Malibu Canyon for the bacteria that pollute Malibu Creek and Lagoon. Almost ten years after incorporation Malibu is still operating with the temporary zoning laws written by volunteers immediately after we declared home rule, and we have yet to develop our Local Coastal Plan, the state-mandated document that defines how the community intends to protect the coastal resources in our care.

When the antidevelopment trio of Carolyn Van Horn, Joan House, and Walt Keller swept into office in 1996 against planning commissioner Barbara Cameron and former school board member Mary Kay Kamath, it seemed logical to ask the defeated slate to assess its loss. Although Van Horn and House were both incumbents, and Keller had served as Malibu's first mayor, many in the community were beginning to talk of a more balanced city council, which made moderates Cameron and Kamath appear to be shoo-ins. The scuttlebutt around town had been that the Hollywood vote—residents who work in the entertainment industry and draw water locally—had once again been influential. A second scenario had it that the voting block from Malibu's two mobile home parks had once again come out solidly for Keller, Van Horn, and House, based on the trio's assurances the land beneath their coaches would not be rezoned for single-family houses.

Cameron and Kamath had run on a platform of constructive compromise, and based on this, their opponents painted them as fellow travelers eager to sit down with developers and give away the store. Kamath, a graduate of Yale Divinity School and a forty-year resident of Point Dume, took a philosophical view. What she wanted for the time she hoped to serve on the city council was to secure the town's long-term financial stability and heal the divisiveness the antidevelopment schism had caused within the community. "Dialogue," said Kamath: dialogue with landowners and people the community referred to as developers, which would lead to negotiation, which would make it possible to develop compromise, an approach Kamath had found effective in her work on the school board. And in any case, wouldn't we be better off with a government that was "experienced, thoughtful, and open-minded?"

"When you're not something, it's hard to prove." Barbara Cameron's eyes lost focus as she reworked the dynamic of her foiled election bid. Cameron had been a single mother in 1979 when she convinced the school district to lease an empty classroom building on Point Dume for a community center and then did the work of applying for permits and securing funds to get the center up and running. The park and jogging track residents constructed to complete the project were named in Cameron's honor. But if Cameron, like Kamath, wasn't prodevelopment, as her opponents painted her, what exactly did she did stand for? If negotiation and compromise (here Cameron and Kamath were speaking literally as opposed to in code) had worked successfully elsewhere, where were the examples? If it is true, as experts on decision-making suggest, that people judge the likelihood something will happen by how many examples in their immediate environment they can call to mind, a quick look around southern California was more than enough to verify what comes of allowing developers to go around unleashed.

And if Cameron and Kamath didn't sound like developers, they didn't sound classically slow-growth either. In fact the team had two problems. First, they were advocating a concept, a multifaceted approach to guide Malibu's development (as opposed to the antidevelopment candidates' insistently one-note campaign), and in this they were attempting to sell the most difficult of political commodities: process. Second, their vision for Malibu was positive. Seasoned problem-solvers and resolutely solution-minded, they anticipated that their job as council members would be to identify problems (as opposed to issues), analyze situations so they might be evaluated (rather than laying blame), then research and implement an expedient course of action. If they expected to make any political hay from what they did, it was that once voters understood what could be accomplished, they would rally around them.

But although the two women were dedicated volunteers whose work had benefited the community, they invoked no models of how they saw themselves functioning as council members. When you ask someone to take a risk, you must provide a good reason to do so. Research on decision-making suggests people need strong inducement to gamble on new ways of doing things but will expose themselves to sometimes terrible risks to avoid suffering a loss. Both Cameron and Kamath complained that even people who knew them personally were swayed by fraudulent newspaper ads claiming their campaign was bankrolled by developers (the Malibu Bay Company—who else was there?). And although the two moderates failed to present examples of situations where compromise and negotiation had worked, their opponents took no chances. Keller, Van Horn, and House produced a video that featured computer animation to model high-density projects the script insisted Cameron and Kamath supported, then distributed cassettes of the program throughout the community just days before the election. "For every inch we moved to convince voters of our long-term commitment to this community and our anti-big-development stand, they threw us back a foot with their fear-and-fiction campaign," Cameron said. But she missed the point: there were examples in the community from the county's watch that validated the fears the antidevelopment trio were playing to.

Lacking a facility with the Code, which in any case represented a negativity that both women found objectionable, Cameron and Kamath were unable to describe the brave new world they anticipated. And although at the time of their run for city council, the final resolution of projects such as Trancas Field was on hold, at least nothing had been built—as antidevelopment advocates lost no time pointing out.

The town's one example of negotiation and compromise, the deal Jeff Jennings developed with Los Angeles County to repair Kanan Dume Road, was two years in the future.

"We had lots of people who were very strong supporters who knew we were absolutely committed to this," said Cameron. "But in the end the video swayed them."

Our stop at Angela and Ben Stewart's house during our progressive Christmas dinner hadn't been planned, but was sandwiched between the main course at Kate and Larry's and dessert at Bill and Natalie's (in my mind, these names run together, Kate-and-Larry, Bill-and-Natalie, Barbara-and-Bob). I was probably not the only one who thought one more glass of wine before dessert was too much, but Angela wanted us to see her Christmas tree. My photographs from the evening show the Stewarts' house done up in high country style, a small ranch house dolled up with checkered wallpaper and pine furniture, the kind of full-flushed homeness I once wished for.

The house was dark except for the Christmas lights, and we all seemed to go in and out of focus like characters out of Dickens. In the muted light, the red in Lee Washington's red-and-white quilted skirt and Kate's red blouse took on a more vivid hue. Sitting on the sofa next to Kate, Betty North's Christmas necklace winked back the blinking lights of the Christmas tree. Ben Stewart popped open bottles of merlot, and the conversation trudged along in fits and starts, more aimlessly now than at the beginning of the evening. We had eaten pasta and cheese and bread at Kate and Larry's, and our minds were with our bellies digesting the food.

Natalie had set out sixteen ironstone dessert plates on the butcher-block island in the center of her kitchen, with a miniature brass candle-holder fitted with a red candle clipped to each plate. Red candles also lighted the rough pine kitchen table, which was loaded with sweets. In suspenders and a Christmas plaid shirt Bill greeted each of us at the front door as Natalie dished out portions of Key lime pie. The married couples took their plates and coffee into the den, leaving the unescorted women to gather at the pine table in the kitchen. Conversation floated toward holiday plans, what to do with the grandchildren, which of us were going to the mountains this year. The men sat comfortable around Bill's fire in the den, slouched on couches and in armchairs, surveying the full life their labor had helped make possible.

Another image: spring this time. I slip in the back door of Duke's restaurant, the old Malibu Sea Lion, refurbished and named for the legendary Hawaiian surfer Duke Kahanamoku, whose sport helped put Malibu on the map. I am late for a chamber of commerce mixer. Inside the restaurant, one of the Malibu Bay Company partners, already in line for the buffet, asks as he does each time I see him if I've found a place to keep sheep to train my dogs. The owner of Beau Rivage restaurant makes his way around the salad bar, taking discreet, teaspoon-sized samples of salsa and potato salad. "Hello, dear," he says absently, recognizing me as a customer. The new city manager, a celebrity since he's been on the job for only two months, is vague in answer to my questions about when Malibu might expect funds to repair the old Rindge pier.

In the dining room I sit across from May Rindge's great-grandson, who looks more like a Duke's waiter in shorts, Hawaiian-print shirt, and neat, short hair. I see Barbara Cameron across the room. She nods and puts her left hand to her ear to tell me she'll call before she leaves for her ranch in Baja. Standing in line for iced tea, I speak to Mary Lou Blackwood, the director of the chamber of commerce, outfitted today in a pink jogging suit and matching pink pearls, her version of beach chic on this bright spring day. When I take my place again at the table, real estate agent and property-rights zealot Tom Bates stops to give me a lead he thinks I should investigate.

Slowly the forks and knives quiet, the small talk diminishes. Malibu's public works director rises and moves to the podium to provide an update on the repair of Kanan Dume Road. I hear the sound of the surf through open windows and feel the slight rustle that will soon become Malibu's two o'clock breeze. The early-season sun warms the room, and I find it difficult to concentrate on the figures the public works director ticks off so deftly about the amount of dirt being stockpiled for the time when Malibu reconciles with Los Angeles County to repair the road. The restaurant, once famous for Josie the sea lion, who lived in one of the tanks "Poppy" Polis built to keep his fish fresh, sits close to the water. Only a low riprap breakwater separates us from the waves. We are on a ship, all of us, on vacation in an ideal climate, entertained by a celebrity.

The public works director winds up his presentation, the meeting concludes. A woman who makes it a point to keep up with things around town stops to tell me how she enjoyed writing a letter to the editor supporting my coverage of a planning commission meeting, which an antidevelopment commissioner had taken issue with. In the parking lot, I wave to the consultant who is engaged in a losing battle on behalf of May Rindge's granddaughter to build a hotel on her share of what's left of the old Rindge rancho. He has also spent time trying to find a place for me to keep sheep and breaks into a wide grin when he sees the Ram logo on my truck hood. I smile, wave again, and turn left out of the parking lot into a quiet eighty-degree weekday afternoon, the kind of day the restaurateurs from Hawaii must have had in mind when they refurbished Josie's old habitat and named it Duke's, forever linking Malibu with blond-haired surfer boys and lazy summer afternoons.

This is the last perfect spring I will spend in this place. We are headed into another city council election, and antidevelopment activists have already begun their letter-writing campaign. I have become a player this time, a role I might have welcomed three years earlier. People stop me at city hall or at council meetings, they slap me on the back and tell me they enjoy what I write or bend my ear with their latest difficulty, like supplicants pleading a case. But they overvalue my importance. We speak of protecting Malibu's way of life, of keeping the community the way it is. For some, this means smogless sun, black skies at night, and a slower pace. The problem is the funnel. For people who work every day in the city, one foot is always stuck where it doesn't belong, one coming, the other going. Worse than the smog and the glare of city lights is the urban grit that now litters the community, brought in on the soles of those for whom the journey out has become a commute. In the old days, the grail for those of us privileged enough to leave the city behind was the potential for enlightenment, the opportunity to shed dead skins. Not just the clean air and the sea and the dark skies at night, but the chance to be renewed and fulfilled and something better than when we began the trip.

In 1999 I am almost a year removed from Malibu, former planning commissioner Harry Barovsky has served one year of his four-year term on the Malibu City Council, and former mayor Jeff Jennings is a year into retirement from civic life. Now settled on the northern slope of the Santa Monica Mountains just over their sandstone crest from Point Dume, I hear from friends that last year's difficult El Niño winter closed Pacific Coast Highway for nine months while repairs skyrocketed to five million dollars. A year earlier a celebration called "Hands across the Parkland" had commemorated the twentieth anniversary of the Santa Monica Mountains National Recreation Area, and a coalition of environmental organizations—Heal the Bay, the Santa Monica Baykeeper, and the Natural Resources Defense Council—successfully sued the Environmental Protection Agency to develop water standards and enforceable cleanup plans for all of Los Angeles and Ventura Counties' most polluted waters, including Malibu Creek. The same year (1998), the California Coastal Commission approved the university the Japanese Buddhists plan for the Santa Monica Mountains. The commission's approval authorized far fewer than the 3,500 students the Buddhists in Tokyo had in mind but left the door open for the university to apply again in twenty-five years, frustrating opponents, who in any case have their hands full fighting the three-thousand-home, two-golf-course Ahmanson Ranch development, revitalized since Seattle-based Washington Mutual bought the property and announced plans to proceed at full speed. Closer to home, Our Lady of Malibu School recently celebrated its fortieth anniversary with John Merrick and Ronald Rindge in attendance, and a house in Malibu which sold two years ago for $965,000 was on the market a year later—with no improvements—for $1,200,000.

In this last year of the twentieth century, I read in *The Malibu Times* that the Los Angeles Regional Water Quality Control Board has threatened to fine the City of Malibu for its "failure to submit a work plan for a technical investigation of water quality impacts from septic systems in areas adjacent to Malibu Creek and Lagoon," and that the city council's immediate reaction was to meet in closed session to consider the possibility of "contesting that action in court." Malibu is waiting on results from yet another study of the creek and the lagoon, this one undertaken by UCLA, and past experience suggests that the city's leaders hope the university's scientists will establish once and for all that Malibu's septic systems are not a source of pollution of the creek and the lagoon, and that the Las Virgenes Municipal Water District's wastewater treatment facility upstream most certainly is. I learn from the newspaper that the California legislature is considering a bill that would mandate statewide minimum discharge standards for on-site sewage treatment systems in the state's coastal zone, and that Malibu's response has been to send a delegation north to Sacramento to insist on an amendment that will insure flexibility in establishing local septic system standards. Later I read that the city has revised its strategy and will now oppose the bill outright. Dave Kagon, gray-haired veteran of the civic center advisory committee, insists the standards the state is considering will result in the closure of almost all of Malibu's septic systems whether they are operating properly or not. It occurs to me (as it has many times in the past) that money spent for studies and lawsuits could be better spent subsidizing purchase of citywide state-of-the-art septic systems or, even better, neighborhood-wide self-contained sewage treatment plants, and so relieve the community of these recurrent altercations with outside agencies.

Still later I read that Malibu's city attorney has announced that the Los Angeles Regional Water Quality Control Board has decided not to fine Malibu, preferring to work with city government to safeguard the water quality in the creek and lagoon, and so avoid a costly legal battle. The city attorney, employing the military jargon that has come to typify such situations, claimed "victory." Again one senses that the two public agencies are working at cross-purposes, the aim of the water quality control board being to identity the source of pollution in prized aquatic landmarks located in Malibu, so that the pollutants can be re-

duced or eliminated, and the community's goal being to prove that septic tanks don't pollute, thereby guaranteeing the sanctity of the septic-
tank rationale for forestalling development. In the end, the city council
will "reluctantly" agree to allocate funds for the study the water quality
control board is requiring, but not without first accusing members of the
board's staff of an anti-septic-tank bias. In one of her typically sweeping
generalizations, Councilwoman Van Horn blames the pollution at
Surfrider Beach, four hundred yards west of where Malibu Lagoon empties into the ocean (and a location routinely noted for poor water quality), on what she identifies as "the grading" in the area. Councilwoman
House wants to know if the study will differentiate between human and
animal contamination. Isolationist Walt Keller objects to the city's having
to underwrite the cost of the research, and rookie councilman Harry
Barovsky worries that if this investigation fails to turn up the type of data
the water quality control board appears to be looking for, the agency will
require yet another study. Thus do some things change and many others
stay the same.

More News from the Front

. . . .

> We live in all we seek. The hidden shows up in too-plain
> sight. It lives captive on the face of the obvious—the people,
> events and things of the day—to which we as sophisticated
> children have long since become oblivious.
>
> Annie Dillard, *For the Time Being*

2000

Big news: Jeff Jennings has reclaimed his seat on the Malibu City Council, and incumbents Walt Keller and Carolyn Van Horn have lost their bid
for reelection (this is the first time Van Horn has not served the citizens
of Malibu as a council member since the community incorporated). I
learn from friends that former planning commissioner and unsuccessful
city council candidate Barbara Cameron was instrumental in the successful Jennings campaign, which was staffed in part by veterans of the
Re-Open Kanan coalition. A front-page headline in *The Malibu Times*
alerts me to Assembly Bill 988, a newly passed state law that requires the
California Coastal Commission to take the unprecedented step of developing a Local Coastal Plan for Malibu. The city has been working on
its own plan, which state law requires of all communities in the coastal
zone, for over six years but so far has been unable to produce a document the commission feels comfortable certifying. I also read, sadly, that
Councilman Harry Barovsky, who was known to consider public service
"a necessity in life," has died in office. His wife, Sharon, has been ap-
pointed to fill his council seat, pending a special election. Later I read
that Sharon has defeated the one candidate who ran against her, a member of the Sierra Club. I also note an editorial by publisher Arnold York

in support of the spirit of conciliation he observes on the newly reconfigured Malibu City Council.

2001

I once took it for granted that communities that established a certain look or fabricated design restrictions as a means to control development were creating something artificial—even as I might find such places attractive. I think of Carmel and the towns of California's Napa Valley, some of the old gold rush communities, certainly Santa Barbara. In the town where my mother lives on Cape Cod, residents are not allowed to change the exterior of their houses without approval from town authorities, which are notoriously biased toward tradition. Driving along Route 6A, the Massachusetts highway that meanders along the Cape's north shore, one is comforted by a sense of stability and of permanence. It is obvious that people have long been established here, taking sustenance from the land and building a foundation for generations that will follow. The town's design restrictions help manifest history in present time, offering physical proof of a long legacy of human settlement that establishes traditions for generations of new residents to meld with their own vision and values.

Across the mountains from Malibu in Agoura Hills, there is a neighborhood determined to maintain just such ties to its past. Old Agoura was once sheep and cow pasture, and some of the structures where residents make their homes have been jury-rigged around old ranch buildings. Crossbars typical of western ranches are built over the two roads that provide access to the community, evoking the area's heritage. A public horse arena with exercise corrals and shade trees and spectator bleachers is the neighborhood's centerpiece. The land the horse facility now occupies was once an empty field, but you don't hear anyone complaining about the loss of open space. The facility is available for individual training and lessons, and for exhibitions and competitions. The arena is also the neighborhood's symbol of itself, and makes a statement about the community's values: the arena and the horse fences and the bridle trails that fan out in three directions are about empowerment. The people who live in this neighborhood have demanded a say in what can be built in proximity to their homes and what new construction will look like. A senior-living facility that might have been just another beige, stucco-sided building was constructed instead with clapboard siding and square-paned windows in keeping with the architectural style of Old Agoura's past.

It is in this manner that a community's built environment, thoughtfully planned and with its design properly executed, can draw residents together and in times of crisis or confusion can be a source of healing. This includes not only buildings, but parks and trails and walkways that help establish the patterns that bring a community together. A well-thought-out built environment provides a community something to act on behalf of and can function not only as a symbol of the community's values, but also as the process by which what is constructed is birthed—the brainstorming, the consensus-building, the positive thinking brought forward to physical fruition—a dynamic that is similar to the way Hana's table functioned as a corporeal symbol of the emotional community shared by those of us who gathered around it. It is difficult to imagine this connection being established if we had chosen instead to sit on the velvet sofas that faced each other across Hana's living room, with all that empty space between us, a void that would have emphasized the otherness that surely lurked among us.

What would Malibu discover if it consulted its past? The Rindge family, certainly, and especially Frederick Hastings Rindge and his appreciation for the spiritual healing available in nature; May Rindge and her Malibu Potteries, another gift from the land and a symbol of ingenuity in the face of adversity; the Hollywood movie colony and surfing (one more gift of nature: world-class waves) and their joint heritage of recreation and health; the resourcefulness of the Chumash and the perseverance of their modern descendants. With skillful architectural rendering, any one of these themes could lend itself to the task of cementing community identity. But one look around Malibu and you are taken aback at how little the ranch motif has been exploited to remind the community of its common past, how little the tiles once produced here have been used as a design motif to infuse the community with a sense of its unique identity—or the culture and workmanship of the Chumash, California's most skillful Native artisans. How little even the beach and surfing culture (the ocean being Malibu's most obvious physical artifact) have been utilized to inspire cohesion.

Representatives from Malibu are again headed north to Sacramento, this time to persuade legislators the community should be allowed to develop its own plan for protecting its coast. But the pleas of the city's delegation appear to have fallen on deaf ears as lawmakers complain that Malibu has dragged its feet too long. The legislators have had it with complaints from constituents about the community's land-use policies. Confronted now by the ultimate nudge forward (this is the first time the Coastal Commission has been put to the service of developing a local municipality's coastal protection policies), Malibu officials are rushing to cobble together a version of a plan from the bits and pieces that have emerged from more than six years of meetings and 210 public hearings, the hope being that the Coastal Commission will consult Malibu's draft as it completes it own document. As the newspaper describes it, Malibu residents are most concerned about how much public beach access the state will require and the number of visitor-serving facilities it might have in mind. Another concern is Malibu's civic center, which the commission apparently views as languishing from a lack of local direction. Joan House, now in her third term on the city council, has described the Coastal Commission's vision for Malibu as less of "an exclusive, private bedroom community" and more of a "visitor friendly destination" equipped with hotels, bed-and-breakfast inns, and restaurants—as if there is nothing in the community's past behavior that might suggest such a conclusion, no long-running feud about beach parking on Point Dume, no squabbles about facilitating public access to beaches along Malibu's twenty-seven miles of coast (the longest stretch of coastline in the care of any municipality in the state). In contrast, the draft plan Malibu's volunteers have put forward, and which town officials are attempting to massage, encourages "passive" use of the coast and suggests recreational use should be "low intensity."

I hear that Coastal Commission executive director Peter Douglas (whom the publisher of *The Malibu Times* has charged with "anti-Malibu bias") and its chair, Malibu resident Sara Wan, have declined to meet with community representatives to discuss the substance of the plan the commission staff is working on—and that Councilman Jeff Jennings, once a voice of reason among the city council's antidevelopment majority, speaks of e-mails that document Malibu's accusations about the commission's failure to respond to the city's overtures as if he is in possession of evidence documenting treason or national threat. Later I learn Malibu has at last managed to deliver a plan, but the Coastal Commission has put it on the shelf. Still later that the commission has issued its own plan, to loud objections from the community, and finally that the city council has called a special meeting to consider what the commission has developed, whereat the usual suspects came forward to charge that if the commission's ideas are implemented, the community will face citywide sewers, affordable housing, more traffic on PCH, and unlimited coastal access.

Councilman Jennings has called the commission's plan "as significant a threat as any natural disaster." Another council member has urged Malibu residents not to vote for any gubernatorial or legislative candidate who supports the Coastal Commission's vision for the community. Still another front-page story informs me that state senator Sheila Kuehl has suggested both parties get together and stop arguing about who's in charge. "It's about finding a real solution," says Kuehl, who seems to appreciate what I suspect, which is that while Malibu may have dropped the ball, the commission may have gone overboard in attempting to rectify the situation. In any event, its plan seems to have offended on all counts, calling for development in the civic center in the manner Councilwoman House fears, while at the same time restricting what can be built elsewhere by redefining much of Malibu as environmentally sensitive. (I recall that during the debate about Malibu's General Plan, antidevelopment activists were much enamored of the term "ESHA" and how it struck fear in the hearts of their property-rights counterparts.)

It has been ten years since the community declared its intention to manage its own affairs, and it has yet to develop goals or strategies to address issues residents insist they are concerned about. What, for example, does the community mean when it refers to slow growth? What policies might residents have in mind—so many houses (or stores or restaurants) this year, more or less or the same the next—and what long-term rationale sustains such thinking? What resources is the community prepared to commit to enforce whatever land-use standards it develops? What provisions might be practical for reviewing and altering policy in the face of changing circumstances? How does Malibu expect to remain financially solvent and maintain whatever slow-growth policies it settles on, especially since what the community appears to mean by slow growth seems antithetical to any kind of growth except single-family homes? And what in fact is the community's policy in regard to the size and intent of this favored mode of development: are estate homes the goal? What did Patt Healy have in mind for the five-acre parcels she lobbied for in Trancas Field—that people would develop the land for ranches and raise horses? And if so, what would residents in the subdivision across the road, or neighbors already ensconced in urban-style mansions nearby, have to say about barns and manure? Do community leaders expect residents will remain indefinitely content to shop, seek entertainment, and secure medical and professional services at a distance with traffic on PCH getting worse as surrounding areas develop?

One is struck by how Malibu's physical layout has influenced the community's political thinking. The geography suggests isolation and withdrawal, cresting a hill and with relief descending into Shangri-la. And although Malibu has been successful in protecting itself against the invasive development typical of southern California, it is one in spirit with the walled and guarded subdivisions where people live behind locked gates, attempting to replicate the isolated exclusivity Malibu projects. Malibu is but one among many secluded outposts where residents have established themselves in dramatic landscapes where they speak of individuality and independence. But by its visibility and its stubborn exclusivity, Malibu holds out the false hope that this kind of escape is warranted, is possible, and can be guaranteed. And with little regard to consequences.

And Malibu has, in fact, developed. There are nearly twice as many people living along this narrow stretch of coast as during the days I spent weekends at my friend Hana's. Today there are three shopping centers where residents can buy trendy clothes and eat in upscale restaurants, when thirty years ago the area lacked even a supermarket. When John Merrick settled in Malibu, children were rounded up in wood-paneled station wagons and dropped at the Las Flores Inn to await buses to take them to their classes in Santa Monica. Today Malibu has two middle schools and a high school. Today in Malibu there is hardly a stretch of beach without a house blocking access to the sand, and Point Dume—bare of landscaping when Hana and her husband settled there in the 1960s—is cluttered with tennis courts and swimming pools and guest-houses, all protected behind locked gates. There is also the fact that despite the environmental rhetoric, the community has set aside no additional land as parkland or wildlife habitat. In fact the amount of open land in Malibu has decreased as top-heavy mansions clutter the hillsides, and the condition of resources such as Malibu Creek and Malibu Lagoon continues to deteriorate.

Of all the people who influenced public life of Malibu I think most often of John Merrick. There is first the manner in which the judge aligned himself with Malibu's setting, so that actions he took on behalf of his personal well-being also benefited the community, which in any case he saw as all of one piece, the landscape and the human population. There was the manner in which Merrick's life was firmly and comfortably set in place, as if he were born to this setting instead of an outsider like me, and how he took his environment straight, unmediated by claims to a higher moral ground. There was Merrick sitting with his wife, Marge, in a pew on the left-hand side of Our Lady of Malibu Church, and the portrait in oils of Judge Merrick in the Malibu court-room named in his honor. There are the three books of Malibu history that citizen Merrick penned and the photograph of young, clean-shaven John Merrick in blue jeans rolled at the cuff and a plaid shirt, pipe casually in his mouth, with long-haired Constantin Rodin, the hermit of Solstice Canyon, the two men sitting on a bench close enough together to suggest more than a passing acquaintance. Many years later, there is John Merrick as master of ceremonies at the dedication of California Landmark No. 965 on Point Dume, commemorating the history he documented, with costumed participants as Captain George Vancouver and Franciscan Francisco Dumetz. There is the retired judge, late in life, observing that it is not development that will ruin Malibu but "the steady encroachment of issues."

The image that presents itself is a circle, round, full, and complete, a symbol of process and of wholeness and of belonging, evidence that an assemblage of disparate parts might be brought together and made to function. Circles connote the movement by which cause becomes effect, and in doing so suggest that what's begun tends toward completion.

I didn't know what I was looking for when I left Los Angeles, nor what I wanted to accomplish when I went to work for *The Malibu Times*. In Malibu I was forced to confront flaws in my own thinking, the most troubling of which was my tendency to think in categories and to arrange these categories into obvious opposites. Without realizing it, I had developed a philosophy that insisted the substance of a circumstance or person or opinion was best understood in relation to its most direct antithesis. In this stiff and shallow taxonomy, elements existed in such unequivocal contradiction to each other that for one to be true, the other had to be false or invalid: *manmade-natural, developer-environmentalist, them-us.* Gradually it came to me that it might not be in the opposites that I would discover the truth I was seeking, but in the middle ground between them. I began to think of this middle ground as a spring that separated the opposites at the same time it bound them together, and that if I forced myself to focus on the place where the spring exerted equal tension, I might discover clues to the circumstances that vexed me, as well as guidance about how to proceed.

This first assumption deflated, I confronted the unrest I felt, as persistent as a low-grade fever, the nervous quivering that had driven me from East to West, from a small town to the city, from the city to what I imagined as country: a disorder I attributed to my failure to be settled in the right place. Thinking this way, I confused place with lifestyle, as if I might pass through a gate and be handed a map and a list of instructions. Again without realizing it, I believed that the way people live in a landscape defines it, even when they disregard the climate and landforms and vegetation that existed before they arrived (all better indicators of how a place should be settled).

Finally, I confronted a third assumption that had limited me: Once my universe was ordered, with all my opposites lined up and me settled in my chair by the fire, I would make what I had established permanent. I would hold on tightly to what I developed, construct blocks all around, and then carefully scrutinize those I allowed in. Set in one place so my roots were lateral as well as deep, I would be free. Gradually I realized this could not be. I forced myself to admit that the change I sought so fervently to avoid must be accepted as a given, and I must step up to meet it. I accepted that I must constantly test the place where the tension in the spring seems the most difficult to bear and jettison my conviction that everything that annoys me can be fixed in accordance with my personal timetable and expectations. Only if I acknowledge what is actually occurring around me and resist the temptation to idealize the circumstances in which I find myself will I progress toward the meaningful life I imagine.

John Merrick was not at Mass the Sunday a priest from the local Franciscan community attempted to explain the Beatitudes as the basis for Christian morality (*Blessed are the poor in spirit, Blessed are they who mourn, Blessed are they who hunger and thirst for righteousness* . . .).

Father Michael suggested dividing the term into its components, *be* and *attitude*, an approach he assured us would make it possible for each of us to develop a better perspective on who we are as individuals and how to function constructively in the situations in which we find ourselves. Wisdom was the goal of the enterprise, Father Michael counseled, and this required a self-critical assessment of our individual strengths and shortcomings.

I thought long and hard about what Father Michael said that morning, hoping to find in his homily a clue to how I might have approached Malibu on a more constructive footing. But in attempting to rework the

Beatitudes in a way that might help me appreciate the morality in their admonitions, I found my thinking jaded: Shame on you, those who mourn (I wagged a finger)—for fear of what you might lose. Shame, too, on the meek, afraid to take a chance. But blessed, oh how blessed are those peacemakers—those among us who find virtue in the middle of the road.

I went to Malibu a white-robed ascetic, feet shod in sandals, so raw-boned at first I never thought to pay homage. Gradually I transformed myself from a bruised and battered pilgrim to a creature tentatively on the wing. Although envisioning the grace of an egret, I was more like a ratty eagle with torn feathers, too long shut in at the zoo. Suddenly free, navigating on faulty instincts, I needed not only practice but a flight plan. Today, offerings made, I am more sure of my mecca, bells and cymbals clanging.

In my worst nightmares, I am closed and disconnected, locked up, cold. I am worn down. I have thoughts but no conclusions, force but no direction, ideas without names. The tattered feathers flash but takeoff is aborted. I have become ungrateful and forget to offer sacrifice. In my best dreams, I am outside. The day is bright and the sun has a glint to it, a sharpness in its light. The wind is clean and I feel direction in the air. A bolt of lightning straightens my spine and I begin to move. . . .

Disaster relief

Total dollars paid to Malibu to recover from six years of disasters, 1992–1998: $16 million (this for a population of 13,000). Emergencies included: Old Topanga wildfire (1993); Northridge earthquake, winter floods (1994); winter floods (1995); Calabasas wildfire (1996); El Niño winter storm and flooding (1998).

Previous major Malibu fires

1930	Potrero; 15,000 acres
1935	Latigo/Sherwood; 28,599 acres
1938	Topanga; 16,500 acres
1943	Woodland Hills; 15,300 acres
1949	Susana; 19,080 acres
1955	Ventu; 12,638 acres
1956	Sherwood/Newton; 37,537 acres, 120 homes, 1 death
1958	Liberty; 17,860 acres, 107 homes
1970	Wright; 31,000 acres, 403 homes, 10 deaths
1978	Kanan Dume; 25,000 acres, 230 homes, 2 deaths
1982	Dayton Canyon; 54,000 acres, 74 homes

Major Pacific storms causing flooding and coastal erosion in Malibu

1934   30-foot breakers

1939   runoff from the inland mountains caused the Army Corps
       of Engineers to armor the Los Angeles River; Malibu Creek
       bridge lost in Malibu

1941   20-foot breakers, winds up to 40 miles an hour

1969   record runoffs, slides, floods, and coastal erosion

1978   most severe coastal erosion in 40 years

1980   slides and beachfront erosion

1983   erosion and runoff worse than the 1941 storm

1988   mudslides and flooding

1992   Malibu's first storm as an incorporated city

The Santa Monica Mountains National Recreation Area

The 150,000-acre SMMNRA, which includes the entire city of Malibu, its 27 miles of coastline, and the mountains that surround the community (Malibu is the only city in the nation completely surrounded by a national park), was established by an act of Congress in 1978. Although 90 percent of the recreation area remains undeveloped, more than 75,000 acres within its boundaries are privately owned. The recreation area is home to 23 federally listed threatened or endangered plant and animal species, 3 listed by the state of California as threatened or endangered, and 46 animal and 12 plant "species of concern." The diverse ecosystem of the mountains is home to 26 distinct natural communities, among which are freshwater aquatic habitats, oak woodlands, valley oak savannahs, and chaparral. Mediterranean evergreen broadleaf forest is the rarest of the earth's biomes; the climate that supports this complex of vegetation occurs in only four areas of the world outside the Mediterranean, including central Chile, south/southwestern Australia, South Africa, and southern California. The SMMNRA differs from other national recreation areas in that people live and work within its boundaries, and unlike other national parks where long-term residents are considered in-holders whose land will eventually be acquired, the residents of the SMMNRA are considered "neighbors and stakeholders."

SOURCES AND ACKNOWLEDGMENTS

On California history: Kevin Starr's multivolume series on California published by Oxford University Press: *Americans and the California Dream* (1973), *California in the Progressive Era* (1985), *Material Dreams: Southern California through the 1920s* (1990), *Endangered Dreams: The Great Depression in California* (1996), and *The Dream Endures: California Enters the 1940s* (1997). Also: *Southern California: An Island on the Land* (Salt Lake City: Peregrine Smith Books, 1973) by Carey McWilliams, who lived the years he writes about; Marc Reisner, *Cadillac Desert: The American West and Its Disappearing Water* (New York: Penguin, 1993); Remi A. Nadeau, *The Water Seekers* (Santa Barbara: Crest, 1997); Robert F. Heizer and Albert B. Elsasser, *The Natural World of the California Indians* (Berkeley: University of California Press, 1980); Bernice Eastman Johnston, *California's Gabrielino Indians* (Los Angeles: Southwest Museum, 1962); and Bruce C. Miller, *Chumash: A Picture of Their World* (Los Osos, Calif.: Sand River Press, 1988) and *The Gabrielino* (Los Osos, Calif.: Sand River Press, 1991).

About life in Malibu, the following were helpful: Frederick Hastings Rindge, *Happy Days in Southern California,* which was privately published in 1972 and is available from the Malibu Lagoon Museum in Malibu, as are the following three books on Malibu history: *A Brief History of Malibu and the Adamson House, The Malibu Story,* and *The Ceramic Art of the Malibu Potteries, 1926–1932.* Also: Reeves Templeman, *Along the Malibu* (Malibu: The Malibu Times, 1972), and W. W. Robinson and Lawrence Clark Powell, *The Malibu* (Los Angeles: Dawson's Book Shop, 1958). See also various issues of *The Malibu Times,* 1992–2002.

For a variety of views on land use and planning issues: William Fulton, *The Reluctant Metropolis: The Politics of Urban Growth in Los Angeles* (Point Arena, Calif.: Solano Press, 1997); Peter Schrag, *Paradise Lost: California's Experience, American's Future* (Berkeley: University of California Press, 1999); Mike Davis, *City of Quartz* (New York: Vintage, 1992), and *Ecology of Fear: Los Angeles and the Imagination of Disaster* (New York: Metropolitan, 1998). For inspiration on nature and the environment: Mary Austin, *The Land of Little Rain* (1903; reprint, New York: Penguin, 1997), Gary Snyder, *A Place in Space: Ethics, Aesthetics, and Watersheds* (Washington, D.C.: Counterpoint Press, 1995), and *The Practice of the Wild* (New York: North Point Press, 1990); Wendell Berry, *Home Economics* (San Francisco: North Point Books, 1987) and *The Unsettling of America: Culture and Agriculture* (1977; reprint, San Francisco: Sierra Club Books, 1996). On contemporary civic issues in the West: William Kittredge, *Who Owns the West?* (San Francisco: Mercury House, 1996); Daniel Kemmis, *Community and the Politics of Place* (Norman: Oklahoma University Press, 1990), and *The Good City and the Good Life: Renewing the Sense of Community* (Boston: Houghton Mifflin, 1995), David James Duncan, *My Story as Told by Water: Confessions, Druidic Rants, Reflections, Bird-Watchings, Fish-Stalkings, Visions, Songs, and Prayers Refracting Light, from Living Rivers, in the Age of the Industrial Dark* (San Francisco: Sierra Club Books, 2001). For their thoughts on place: Winifred Gallagher, *The Power of Place* (New York: HarperPerennial, 1993), and Scott Russell Sanders, *Staying Put: Making a Home in a Restless Word* (Boston: Beacon Press, 1993). Lewis Mumford provides historical perspective in *The City in History: Its Origins, Its Transformations, and Its Prospects* (New York: Harcourt, Brace & World, 1961). The quotation from Robert Redford comes from "Robert Redford: The Politics and Pleasures of Managing a Western Landscape," *Architectural Digest,* June 1993.

Thanks to Arnold York, publisher of *The Malibu Times,* for allowing me a long leash, thanks to my colleagues at the newspaper, especially Pam Linn. Thanks to former Malibu planning director Joyce Parker-Bozylinski and former city manager David Carmany for reading drafts of the manuscript, and to members of the Malibu city staff who helped me understand how municipalities work. Thanks to Ellen Meloy for encouraging me at the beginning, and to Sandy Crooms for her persistence and understanding as the manuscript progressed. Thanks, finally, to my husband, Andrew O'Malley, who stood firm throughout and provided encouragement.